THE GOSPEL PROJECT

THE GOSPEL
PROJECT

by
Jean-Paul Audet

Translated by
Edmond Bonin

PAULIST PRESS DEUS BOOKS
New York, N. Y.   Paramus, N. J.
Toronto   London

A Deus Books Edition of Paulist Press, originally published under the title *Le projet evangelique de Jesus,* © 1968 by Cahiers de Communaute Chretienne, Montreal, Canada, and Aubier Editions Montaigne, Paris, France.

NIHIL OBSTAT:
Lawrence A. Gollner
Censor Librorum

IMPRIMATUR:
✠ Leo A. Pursley, D.D.
Bishop of Fort Wayne-South Bend

July 4, 1969

The Nihil Obstat and Imprimatur are official declarations that a book or pamphlet is free of doctrinal or moral error. No implication is contained therein that those who have granted the Nihil Obstat and Imprimatur agree with the contents, opinions or statements expressed.

Library of Congress
Catalog Card Number: 79-92921

Published by Paulist Press
Editorial Office: 304 W. 58th St., N. Y., N. Y., 10019
Business Office: Paramus, New Jersey 07652

Printed and bound in the
United States of America

Contents

Preface

In the last few years especially, there has been much talk of the "Gospel event." I myself have spoken about it often. The expression, of course, is not entirely new, but it contains insights whose power of renewal could be immense in the present situation of the Church.

The Gospel is not, first of all, a more or less secret quarry where the liturgy hews the toothing stones for each day's homily. And it is not primarily a collection of texts (usually terribly dislocated) in which we are to seek random scraps of inspiration for our Christian life. Neither is it a closed book whose seals can be broken only by theologians and experts in various fields. What good would that be, when you come down to it? The Church is not an institution of higher learning that lectures on the meaning of the world and of life; her role does not consist in marking out the path to immortality with beacons of sheer knowledge. Nothing would be more contrary to Jesus' intentions and, at the same time, to God's plan than to view the Church thus as a society of lucky escapists.

What really comes first in the Christian community is our baptismal brotherhood, a brotherhood directed toward actively fostering evangelical hope throughout the entire human family. Creating this brotherhood is the great concern of the Gospel. To whatever extent the Christian community fails in the pursuit of this objective, the internal organization of the Church strays from its principal *raison d'être* and runs the risk of seeming, within as well as without, a mere mass of excessive claims, stifling laws and abstract declarations. History is there to remind us that this danger is not an illusion born of groundless fears.

Paul, instead, saw the Gospel as a "power" emanating from the living God and spreading through the world so as to foster universally the highest hope of "life," which is offered without distinction to all "who have faith" (Rom. 1, 16-17). Faith, consequently, was the interior furrow where the message planted the power of the Gospel. What mattered most, afterwards, was the germination of hope, rather than the endless refining of the formulas in which that faith was expressed.

In this perspective, the Gospel retained all its original quality as an event. It was a force which was universally radiated, starting from Jesus, via thousands of channels, before and behind, throughout the whole of mankind's existence. As for the Church, she was that fraternal milieu where the hope of "life," to which the Gospel bore witness, was shared in common, beyond all the divisive factors of old: "There is one Body, one Spirit, just as you were all called into one and the same hope when you were called. There is one Lord, one faith, one baptism, and one God who is Father of all, over all, through all and within all" (Eph. 4, 4-6).

Yet, when we state that the Gospel is an event in the realm of hope before being a book, a doctrine, or even a repertory of arguments justifying the ecclesial institution; when, in this sense, we speak of the "Gospel event," some people start to wonder and others protest impatiently. An event? We have heard this many times already. But accepting such a view of things means locking ourselves in the past, does it not? And, by that very fact, will it not weaken our presence in the world of today? The many more or less nostalgic pictures of the early Christian community which we have seen have left us utterly helpless before the extraordinarily moving realities of contemporary life. This talk of an "event" is all well and good, but those who use the word should realize that it will not exert any magic power over the consciousness of the men and women among whom we live. Therefore, they should also tell us how we can establish continuity between our Christian project, or our pastoral project, on the one hand, and Jesus' evangelical project on the other.

Let us view the matter from another angle. As Christians and priests, we are required to be "present" to the world around us, "present" to the communities nearest us. Again, this is fine. And again, in this connection, we are told of the "Gospel event." But they should start by telling us exactly what Jesus' presence among his people was like and, also, what his presence in the early Christian community was like later. After that, we might be better equipped to fashion for ourselves an effectual "presence" among the men and Christians of today. We do not want recipes, but we believe we have a right to demand that our tradition show us some models. Otherwise, what is the use of speaking to us about a "living" tradition? Now, the models we wish most to know in this regard are Jesus himself and his immediate disciples.

All things considered, it is perhaps not unreasonable to hope that the models thus brought back to the surface—or, more accurately, thrown anew into the mainstream of life—will help us re-establish genuine continuity between our Christian project, or our pastoral project, and Jesus' evangelical project, which is the permanent source of that "Gospel event" in which we know that we are supremely involved right now. At the present time, nothing seems more necessary to us than restoring this living continuity at the crucial level of our various projects. There can be no project, however, unless there are open options and unless the government of the Christian community concretely acknowledges a wide freedom of initiative. Do we have real options yet? Do we have a just and sufficient freedom of initiative? Too often, on the contrary, we at the bottom get the impression that we have become, to all intents and purposes, the remote executors of projects which are invariably and almost wholly situated outside of us—sometimes back there in the past, and sometimes up there in the supreme councils of the power pyramid. Does this situation result from the truth of the Gospel? If not, should it go on indefinitely?

Such were, in substance, the questions which I was invited to answer at the last session (1968) of the Institut de Pastorale in Montreal. Our discussions raised a number of new questions, some of which went to the heart of the problem while others remained more peripheral. Planned beforehand, the publication of the results imposed a fairly difficult choice. I have tried to retain, from the bulk of my contributions, whatever seemed to possess more lasting interest, without yet sacrificing everything which did not strictly fit into a perfectly unified analysis. The result is, as times, a somewhat sinuous composition for which I beg the reader's indulgence. I believe, however, that the subtitles will compensate for the drawbacks inherent in trying to follow the steps of an actual inquiry closely.[1]

Meanwhile, the rather mixed reception given to *Humanae vitae* abruptly brought into the foreground of actuality the entire order of problems with which we are dealing here. Many Christians, both laymen and priests, immediately realized that the point at issue here is not only the divergent views on the lawfulness of using contraceptives, but, even more so, the very mode of each baptized person's integration into the Christian community. What will that mode be? Neither our Christian nor our pastoral project, indeed, can be defined by its mere content. Both are also characterized by a certain way of appropriating the evangelical values. Consequently, what will our obedience be like? Or our fidelity? Our freedom? And how about our manner of governing: will it be a princely administration of the sacred, or will it create a genuinely brotherly community? Before answering these questions, it will surely not be superfluous to take a fresh look at Jesus' evangelical project as well as at the implementation of it inaugurated by his immediate disciples.

J.-P. A.

[1] At this point, I wish to thank the editors of *Communauté chrétienne* most sincerely for allowing me to reprint here the text of the two articles which form the body of this book and which first appeared in *Communauté chrétienne*. (Montreal, 1968), Nos. 38-39, pp. 97-176. The original text, however, has been slightly modified.

I
Jesus among His People

I wonder whether a certain facile familiarity with the Gospel narratives has not led us, insensibly, to consider Jesus' presence among his people as *something established from the start.* To me, this opinion seems quite widespread at all levels of the Christian community. Yet it is hardly ever stated explicitly: derived from habit rather than from reflection, it remains concealed for the most part in the shadows of the unconscious.

For that reason, it is not easy to pinpoint. If I devote time and space to it here, I do so, not for the sheer pleasure of investigation, but because of the grave consequences attendant upon such a view. Indeed, it affects not only the preeminent model of our pastoral activity—the activity of Jesus himself —but also what I shall call the simply Christian take-over of his evangelical project. Either way, the spontaneous mental picture we paint of Jesus' presence among his people profoundly conditions *everything we do to further the hope contained in the Gospel.*

One View of Jesus' Person and Activity

What is our mental picture like? For brevity's

sake, I must make a rather summary generalization, and I apologize; but, despite the limited value of all such generalizations, I still think it will be useful to suggest the following test, which, to my mind, illustrates the point I am trying to make. Listen to our conversations, analyze our homilies, follow the general direction of our catechesis. Most of the time, you will notice, our reading of the Gospel proceeds as if the *person* of Jesus were a *basic* fact, to be taken for granted. As a result, his *activity,* the structure and the very style of it, appear to be just so many natural *consequences* of the unique quality of his person—his person being considered, in every respect, as *given once and for all,* right from the beginning.

An Utterance "Prefabricated" in Silence

Thus, for example, Jesus *speaks,* but we do not really believe that he ever had to *prepare* what he said. Without stating so outright, we seem to think that, from the moment he opened his mouth, he started drawing *directly* and effortlessly from the inexhaustible treasures of divine wisdom. Everything—substance and form—was somehow "prefabricated" for him in the mystery of the person called the "Word." It is as though the parables, among other things, lay ready-made in the luminous secrets of the incarnation. A curious "incarnation," to tell the truth!

Upon questioning, some, I feel sure, would maintain that the only possible preparation for Jesus' speaking was *silence.* And they conjure up the thirty years of "hidden life" in Nazareth. Thus, somehow or other, Jesus' utterance would have taken shape, essentially *outside* the world of utterance. Yet, does not such a notion, however common it may be, seem a trifle strange the moment we reflect on it?

As a matter of fact, who ever thinks of Jesus' utterance *before* the start of his public activity? If we do, we immediately shelter it within the protected circle of the "holy family." An authentic human utterance, with its countless meanderings, its fleeting remarks and its profusion of idle words, does not, in our judgment, seem a sure path to evangelical utterance. We would rather imagine a vast silence punctuated only now and then by useful statements and edifying reflections, all leading directly to the proclamation of that astounding "Good News."

A Fluent Utterance

Jesus' utterance was lucid, daring, uninhibited, stimulating, original, creative. Even in today's atmosphere of controversy and criticism and suspicion, it still manifests extraordinary vitality. But we habitually shut our eyes to the true conditions under which it first gushed forth. According to the image which I am presently trying to bring back to the surface, Jesus' utterance strikes us above all, perhaps, as ready and fluent—an utterance which did not have to find itself, as our does, in the semidarkness of the multitudinous perceptions among which every man must *choose*.

A Crossroads

It would be easy to adduce many such readings of the Gospel event. I shall limit myself to one more example, in order to define this mentality more clearly. After John baptized him in the Jordan, Jesus seems to have gone through a brief period of decisive questioning about himself and his undertaking. His baptism placed him, so to speak, at a sort of crossroads. Early Christian tradition looked upon this crossroads as a "test" *(peirasmos)*, opening onto *orientations* which would determine the deepmost quality of the entire Gospel event.

Our translations have turned this crossroads, this "test," into days of "temptation" in the desert. Not very felicitous, to say the least, this interpretation placed us in a vague atmosphere of threatened virtue, whereas the whole point of the episode was the decisive self-scrutiny of him who would initiate the Gospel event. Actually, we should see Jesus' solitude in the desert as the *hour of great options* preparatory to the carrying out of a vast and perilous plan. It is quite possible, too, that early Christian tradition, from which we hold our accounts, deliberately chose to concentrate into those few days each and every "danger" to which Jesus had personally exposed himself in executing his "mandate."

Why Galilee?

But that is not so much what I wanted to call attention to for now. We read that, after his baptism, Jesus returned to Galilee. This is where he spread his initial message. Like the heralds in antiquity, who officially disseminated news of public interest, he went quickly from village to village, from city to city and, when the opportunity arose, from synagogue to synagogue and house to house. Speaking *in God's name,* he announced, "The time has come, and the kingdom of God is close at hand. Repent, and believe the Good News" (Mk. 1, 14-15; compare Mt. 4, 12-17. 23-25; Lk. 4, 14-15).

But why Galilee? I doubt whether many of us have ever stopped to ponder what this piece of information means. For most readers and listeners, it is a purely anecdotal detail. Jesus chose Galilee. Fine, but what difference does that make? He could have begun anywhere at all, and the Gospel event would have been exactly the same. Furthermore, is it not natural to imagine that if Jesus headed for Galilee first, he was simply going back to his own little country? He would be starting in the localities which he knew and loved best.

Since I do not wish to dally here over a long demonstration, which could soon seem utterly pointless and therefore intolerably pedantic, I shall come straight to the point.

Early Christian tradition certainly did not look upon Jesus' *choice* of Galilee for the inauguration of his activity as a mere anecdotal detail, interchangeable with any other. On the contrary, it looked for a *meaning* in this fact; but it could look for a meaning only because it first saw an option there.

As proof, there is the *topographical* Galilee-Jerusalem pattern throughout Matthew, Mark and Luke. As further and more conclusive proof, there is the prophetic quotation which, in Matthew's account, is intended to underscore the meaning behind Jesus' choice of *Galilee* as the scene of his initial activity:

Land of Zebulun! Land of Naphtali!
Way of the sea on the far side of Jordan,
Galilee of the nations
that is, melting pot of the Gentiles and the Jews!
The people that lived in darkness
has seen a great light;
on those who dwell in the land
   and shadow of death
a light has dawned.

(Mt. 4, 15-16, quoting Is. 8, 23-9, 1)

The Method of the Early Christians

What interests me at present in this search for
a meaning in the fact that Jesus chose Galilee as
the starting point of his activity, is the method the
early Christians used. Indeed, to my mind, it ex-
emplifies a certain reading of the Gospel event
itself. Now, what strikes me most about their
method is the way they *proceeded* from Jesus' *activity* to the concrete *options* which it presupposed,
then from options concerning details to the overall
project into which they entered, and, finally, from
Jesus' overall evangelical project to God's plan,
represented, in our illustration, by the passage
from Isaiah.

Clearly, this is the exact opposite of what we
are so prone to do when we try to understand the
Gospel event. As I pointed out earlier, we instinc-
tively start from the *person* of Jesus, which is
obviously a divine person. His *activity* then flows
from his person with the ease characteristic of
things that work almost automatically. In consequence, we also consider God's plan as a sort of
patent fact which dominates both Jesus' person

and his activity and, thus, the entire course of the
Gospel event.

In my opinion, this is an unfortunate view, with
numerous and far-reaching effects not only on
pastoral work but in every ramification of the
Christian life itself.

A Passive Incarnation

First off, I would say that from the pastoral
standpoint—which is what concerns us here—this
view makes us insensible to the *overall project* and
the *concrete options* which, in point of fact, shaped
Jesus' activity. By the same token, it tends to restrict our vision of the incarnation, more or less
unconsciously, to the moment of Jesus' *birth*—and
even to his mother's "Yes." Is there anything
theologians and preachers have not said about this
wonderful "instant"? Whether we realize it or not,
this line of thinking usually leads us to a sort of
passive incarnation, in which the initial *instant*
that unites two "natures" is perfectly comple-
mented, some thirty years later, by an *obedience*
of the same type—that is, a *passive obedience*.

Instantaneous Obedience

For, in keeping with this interpretation, there
is a strict correlation between what I would call the
style of Jesus' obedience and the style of his birth.
In neither case is there any searching, any real
growth, any development. The style of his obedience is already wholly contained in the style of his
birth. In other words, his birth furnishes the prototype according to which we picture his obedience
and, consequently, the Gospel event itself.

Accordingly, just as his birth tends to be com-
pressed into an *instant,* so his obedience, in turn,
becomes instantaneous, *immediate.* From there on
in, we find ourselves talking about an obedience
which tends to shed the quality of *duration* like
something human (too human!) and unnecessary,
not to mention inglorious. Hence, we are inclined
to consider his obedience *easy*—as easy as his birth,
in fact, because it is really a *passive* obedience, just
as his birth was passive.

Jesus as an Occasion

On this score, the special attention we so often
accord to Mary's "Yes" seems particularly revealing
to me. For one thing, it shows that we experience
no difficulty—quite the contrary!—in contemplating
the evangelical project *outside* of Jesus. With regard to his birth, the evangelical project lies in
his *mother's* "Yes"; with regard to his obedience
as a man, it lies in God's "Yes," which is his
Father's plan. Jesus thus becomes, as it were, the
site, or the *occasion,* of a plan and of an obedience.
But to whatever extent he becomes an occasion,
there is a corresponding obscurement of the fundamental fact that he really *formed* and *carried* the
evangelical project and that his obedience was
truly *his own.*

Our Reading of the Gospel Event

And in all this, of course, we continue our
sincere quest for what we call the "incarnation."
I, for one, doubt whether many of us discover it
efficaciously in our reading of the Gospel event.
We manage to get there with difficulty, only in cer-

tain passages—especially those that deal with suffering: what a symptom!—when we read the accounts by Mathhew, Mark and Luke. Needless to
say, we get there with far greater difficulty, and
much more sporadically, when we read John or
Paul, who offers us still fewer footholds because,
first of all, they both bask more in the glory of
the resurrection.

We Are Ill at Ease in Our Own Humanity

At bottom, we very much *want* Jesus to be
truly God. I am less sure that we are as keen on
his having been truly man. (Still, the equilibrium
of our Christian heritage presupposes an effective
meeting of both perceptions, just at it also presupposes the effective meeting of both facts in the
concrete unfolding of the Gospel event.) The
result is that, in our quest for the incarnation—pref-
erably an *instantaneous* one, which would thereby avoid the diminution of history—we are rather
ill at ease in the presence of an authentic incarnation. Unquestionably, the reason for this is that
*we are ill at ease with our own humanity in the
first place.*

Dimly and without quite admitting it to ourselves, we reject one whole part of the incarnation,
just as we reject one whole part of our human
condition—and, it seems to me, under the influence
of the same deep-rooted drives. This doubtlessly
explains that sort of emptiness which, in us and
in our language, affects the *name* of Jesus—"Jesus
of Nazareth," as the first generation of Christians
loved to say. Conversely, it also explains in part
our spontaneous clinging to a few of Jesus' *titles,*

which, it must be added, we do not fail to treat as
mere *names:* "the Christ," "our Lord," "our Lord
Jesus Christ."

Moreover, it is important to realize that, in all
this ambiguity surrounding our habitual concept
of Jesus' birth and obedience, we are led much
less by strictly theological concerns than by profound *affective* motivations, anterior to any for-
mulation of the Christian heritage. Behind all
this, in short, I believe there is a *fear:* essentially
a *fear of ourselves.*

Accepting Ourselves

Indeed, in order to accept "Jesus of Nazareth"
as he really is, we would also have to be able to
accept *ourselves* as we really are; and conversely,
in order to accept ourselves fully, we must—from a
Christian viewpoint at least—be able to accept
"Jesus of Nazareth," Christ and Lord, in accordance
with the very equilibrium of this formula. In the
Christian economy, these two acceptances go hand
in hand; these two reconciliations are interdepen-
dent. As the history of Christianity has long since
proved, we shall always have trouble speaking about
"Jesus of Nazareth" authentically until each of us,
in his own humanity, has first learned to say *his
own name as a man or a woman* authentically.

*

Without laboring the point, let me simply
state once more why I made the preceding observations. In order to grasp the original mode and
quality of Jesus' presence among his people, it was

necessary to reopen the road to a certain reading of the Gospel event. Though this road is still rather cluttered, I hope that I have helped to remove a few obstacles.

The Example of Our Earliest Witnesses

I undertook this task with all the more tranquillity of mind as the reading to which I am trying to reopen the road, is the very one which presided over the formation of the Christian tradition at the outset. The first stage of that formation is represented for us mainly by the accounts in Matthew, Mark and Luke.

There is no reason to fear that, in saying this, we shall eventually divide our earliest witnesses, with Matthew, Mark and Luke on one side, and John and Paul on the other. On the contrary, we unite them, and in the *only equilibrium* which is proper.

Paul especially—but John also, to a certain extent—speaks to us about Jesus in a manner that *presupposes* the resurrection. Thus, in varying degrees but in great abundance on both sides, we have there a testimony formulated in terms of the *ultimate meaning* of the *situation* that resulted from the Gospel *event* as a whole. Needless to say, this testimony is extremely precious to us in any case.

Familiarization with Jesus of Nazareth

But the *early* unfolding of the Gospel event— with its long periods of waiting, its detours, its foreshadowings, its *partial meanings,* and even its lumpishness—is also of *inalienable value* to us. In the Christian economy, we cannot speak of the "Christ," the "Lord," the "Son of God," the "first to be born from the dead" and the "first-born of all creation" if we neglect to grow deeply familiar, in hope and in faith, with "Jesus of Nazareth."

Now, no witnesses can help us achieve this familiarity with "Jesus of Nazareth" better than Matthew, Mark and Luke. Since I was asked to discuss Jesus' presence among his people, I therefore turned my attention to these three witnesses first of all. Due to a whole complex of factors and circumstances, we generally give the synoptics a cursory reading; but at this time we need to ponder them long and deep. What I have tried to do is map out the road to such a reading a little more fully.

Jesus' Evangelical Project and Our Pastoral Project

Early Christian tradition respected the *beginnings* of the Gospel event. What is more, it appreciated them, savored and loved them. It pored over every detail from Jesus' baptism to his resurrection; and, in proportion as it developed, it was even inclined to keep broadening this concrete basis of the conditions of Jesus' activity. When speaking about that activity, the first generation of Christians used two categories, distinguishing roughly between what Jesus had "done"—not a matter of "good example"!—and what he had "said." These are the two kinds of operation which very explicitly subtend Luke's narrative (Acts 1,1).

The Expansion of Jesus' Activity

The narratives of Matthew, Mark and Luke, it is true, considerably shorten the *time span* of Jesus' activity, reducing it to less than a year, apparently, instead of some three years, as in John's account. But we should notice that they do not narrow the *area* in the same proportion. No doubt, that is because, all things considered, space seemed more significant than time in delimiting the frontiers of Jesus' presence among his people. At any rate, what interests us at the moment is the fact that the first generation of Christians spontaneously wished that, in this space-time, they could leisurely unfurl all the "doing" and all the "saying" in Jesus' activity.

The Import of a Genealogy

There was indeed a profusion of words and actions, but they were arranged from within with a delicate sense of the reality of life. Luke even went so far in this direction as to end up doing a very curious thing: after reporting the inauguration of Jesus' activity, he added something seemingly incongruous—a genealogy (Lk. 3, 23-38; compare Mt. 1, 1-17). What a bizarre notion for a writer who was ordinarily so painstaking!

But, on second thought, what a wealth of suggestion in this very simple technique! What a compendium of authenticity in this seeming delay! The Gospel event was accepted in its *duration:* it possessed an *unfolding,* a *development,* like everything truly human. It had an utimate meaning, but it also had an *initial* meaning—at once necessary and valid—in the early public activity of this "Jesus of Nazareth" who was called the son of Joseph the carpenter. In a word, the Gospel event followed a progression, and *throughout the length of that progression* the first Christians perceived what we call the "incarnation."

The Preduration and Presignificance of the Gospel Event

Moreover, by means of a genealogy (which is nothing but a series of begettals: men and women together!), the Gospel event regained a sort of *preduration*—the preduration that belonged to it by right. At the same time, it acquired a kind of *presignificance.* What human truth! What clarity! And, incidentally, what light it shed on the obscure and ulterior meaning of our lives! That, too —and in the first place—was the "incarnation." In this rich and marvelously concrete perception, the *presignificance* of Jesus' genealogy certainly took nothing away from the *ultimate* meaning of the event: the glorification of that same Jesus henceforth recognized as Christ and Lord.

Neither did the ultimate meaning, under the pretext of his greatness and prestige, clandestinely "devour" the presignificance, as if it had been worthless. On the contrary, the presignificance confirmed the ultimate meaning by *preparing* it. For everything authentically human is prepared in a period of germination. The Gospel germinates in me, and, in a sense, I germinate in it. What have we done with this genealogy of Jesus in theology, in our pastoral work, and in the Christian life pure and simple? We have grown accustomed to skim-

ming over it as if it were more or less of a filler.
Yet, to the first generation of Christians, it was,
beyond a doubt, something far more galvanic.

Jesus' Activity as a Sign

At first, therefore, Jesus' presence among his
people was essentially that of his *activity*. Then this
activity—words, deeds and attitudes (and not only
prodigies!)—was gradually taken as a *global sign*
of the nature of the *person*. The same road eventually led to God's *plan*—not along a direct course,
not in an instant and not in a single breakthrough,
but during the obscure and sinuous processes of
germination.

Mission in the Mind of Jesus

As for Jesus himself, he spoke especially of his
"mission"—or, as he also called it, the "command"
or "will" of his Father. Such was Jesus' understanding. At this point, we must beware of going
astray. God's plan did not present itself to Jesus
like an architect's drawing. Jesus was not some
kind of "engineer" of the kingdom of God. He
did not, with his inner gaze, read the detailed
"blueprint" of the Gospel event while pretending,
with his human eyes, to feel his way along the same
paths as his people. Neither was Jesus a sort of
first-born of monks and seminarians. The Gospel
event was not, for him, like the "customary" of a
novitiate or the "rule" of a seminary.

In actual fact, Jesus was conscious of having
a "mission." This basic insight, to which the first
generation of Christians called attention, must be
given due importance. Since the time of the proph-

ets, Israel knew the meaning of a "mission"
received from God. We have only to think of Hosea,
Isaiah and Jeremiah, among others. To paint a
picture that approximates what I am trying to suggest here, let us say, then, that Jesus' fidelity to his
"mission" was of the *prophetic* type. Such, too, was
his "obedience" to God's plan.

Jesus' Evangelical Program

Now, a "mission" presupposes genuine freedom
of initiative. It presupposes *options*. It presupposes
preparations, experiments, gropings, successes and
failures. It presupposes calculated risks, depending
on what the concrete circumstances of one's activity
dictate to his judgment and wisdom. In more familiar terms, we would say that Jesus carried his
"mission" within himself like a project.

This program took shape in his mind, his consciousness. How could the "incarnation" not have
been there likewise? In this sense, there was, in him,
an *evangelical project*. It was visualized gradually;
it developed. When describing Jesus' childhood and
youth, Luke significantly observes that he *"in-
creased* in wisdom, in stature, and in favor with
God and men" (Lk. 2, 52; compare 2, 40). He does
not say "with" God and "before" men, but, in a
mysteriously and magnificently equal manner,
"with God and men."

Jesus among Us

There! Now we have got our bearings. Jesus
was really *in our midst*. He was really among his
people. Strictly speaking, it is only *in the glory of
the resurrection* that the evangelical project was

fully unveiled to the very one who had carried it
until then. From that moment on, what a change
there was in Jesus' words and manner! What assurance and what peace! We can sense something
of it in all the witnesses as we read the accounts
of the resurrection. In the narrative of the fourth
Gospel, that great paschal radiance *flowed back* in
a particularly noticeable way on Jesus' last conversations with his disciples (Jn. 13-17). This also
explains, from a more general viewpoint, the re-
markably confident and luminous quality of Jesus'
words and deeds in the overall interpretation by
John.

The Evangelical Program and
Our Pastoral Program

I have laid stress on the project which gave
birth to the *Gospel event,* for I believe that the way
we picture it to ourselves concretely is extremely
important in the shaping and implementing of our
pastoral program. Between these two programs
—the evangelical and the pastoral—there must be
continuity not only of content but also, in a sense,
of *style.*

In our present situation, this question of style
is far-reaching. It brings up the whole problem
of *freedom of initiative* and *open options* in the
performance of our pastoral service. It likewise
brings up the whole problem of the *fundamental
character of our obedience and fidelity* in the
Church. Lastly, it brings up the whole problem
of the *"regulating"* of our pastoral activity *from
above.* Putting it tersely, I would ask: Shall we
carry our pastoral program like an architect's plan,

or like a "mission"? In the final analysis, for us as for Jesus, that is the crux of the matter.

What Will Our Fidelity Be Like?

What, consequently, will our fidelity be like? And our obedience? Will our inmost fidelity resemble the engineer's, or the prophet's? Will our activity be governed by the consciousness that we are carrying an architect's plan within ourselves, or will it be inspird by the consciousness that we are sharing responsibility for an authentic program? What shall we have before our eyes—closed options, or open ones? With regard to obedience, shall we attach equal value to mission, mandate and program, on the one hand, and to constitutions, codes and regulations, on the other? In reality, there are *two kinds* of obedience and fidelity, though they are usually confused at all levels in the structure of the ecclesial community. Both kinds are necessary and valuable, but we must understand that *their respective necessity and value are not equal.* In this connection, without the least doubt, mission, mandate and program rank first.

Freedom of Initiative and Open Options

Now, mission, mandate and program *presuppose a just freedom of initiative and a judicious range of options.* The question, then, is whether our initiatives will be carried out in an atmosphere of clandestinity, and whether our options will be approached with a feeling of perpetual delinquence. Correlatively, the question is also whether the various echelons of government in the Christian community will reserve to themselves a freedom

which is all the more exclusive in proportion as
they enjoy a more universal power, or whether,
on the contrary, freedom will be all the broader
in proportion as it more closely conditions concrete responsibility for Christian and pastoral work.

It is altogether wrong and, in a word, *contrary
to the very style of Jesus' evangelical activity*—not
to mention the normal conditions of ordinary human activity—to dispose matters in such a way that
Christian freedom ceaselessly tends to rise toward
the top of the power pyramid. All declarations and
exhortations to the contrary notwithstanding, such
a state of things is an open door to the universal
invasion of regulation and passivity, as well as to
the dangerous primacy of administration over true
government.

The Style of Jesus' Presence among His People

Faced with this sort of questioning, we may
protest and conjure up the specter of excessive
fluidity in the Christian community. Is this being
clear-sighted? Is it truly wise?

> The wind blows wherever it pleases;
> you hear its sound,
> but you cannot tell where it comes from or
> where it is going
> That is how it is with all who are born
> of the Spirit.
>
> (Jn. 3, 8)

In any case, there is nothing more fluid than the
first welcome each of us extends to the hope offered
by the Gospel.

Furthermore, the facts are there, along the
paths of history. They speak for themselves, and

they speak loud. The real style of Jesus' presence among his people cannot be annulled, either by our fears or by our habits. We know what we have to do. There must be no break in continuity between the style of our pastoral program and that of Jesus' evangelical program, nor between the style of Jesus' evangelical program and that of our Christian program. For today's Christian community—and, doubtlessly, even more for tomorrow's—this is the question which comes before all the rest. It is infinitely more important than the beautiful alignments of the power pyramid, which, in general, are purely and simply confused with the real foundations of authority.

Two Models Immediately Ruled Out in Jesus' Activity: The Priest and the Legist

Concretely, as I have already noted more than once, Jesus' presence among his people was first assured by his activity. To revert to the categories used by the early chroniclers, this activity comprised essentially "doing" and "saying": on the one hand, things which belonged to the order of deeds and dealings, and, on the other, things which belonged to the order of the spoken word. At the *immediate* source of this activity, there was Jesus' consciousness of a "mission," a "mandate."

The Style of Jesus' Obedience

All the witnesses agree on this point. They also agree in situating Jesus' obedience here, *first of all.* Along this path—which, as a matter of fact, had

already been mapped out by the prophets of old—
Jesus first saw his evangelical program as the expression and accomplishment of the "plan" or
"will" of *God himself.* His program, in turn, presupposed a certain *style* of implementation. As we
have said, this style called for authentic "incarnation," where there was room for the normal exercise of the various coordinates of human activity,
which is always extended in time and always in-
serted into a history. These coordinates comprised
chiefly reflection, trial, initiative and choice. In
sum, they created the necessary human space where
the *initial* meaning of the Gospel event (that of
the beginnings) was not in constant danger of being obliterated by its *ultimate* meaning (that of
glorification with God).

The Conditions in Which Jesus Began and Carried Out His Activity

At this point, we should undoubtedly let Matthew, Mark, Luke and John tell us what Jesus'
presence among his people was like in the meand-
ering course of time. The general observations
made so far were meant merely to eradicate certain
habits and thus clear the way for a more open
and direct, a more concrete and suggestive, a better balanced and, in a word, *truer* reading of our
Gospel accounts.

Without entering into too many details, I
think it will be useful to pause again for a moment
over the *conditions* in which Jesus inaugurated and
then pursued his activity among his people. The
remarks which we will be led to make on this subject will perhaps correct, in a few particulars, the

very narrow and very abstract ideas we often form
of Jesus' presence among his people.

The Dual Model of Priest and Doctor of the Law

Let us first note two negative conditions which,
without a doubt, both had great bearing on the
style of Jesus' activity. He was never able to count
on the two social models of the "priest" and the
"doctor of the Law" to define himself in the eyes
of his people, to situate and frame his activity and,
at the same time, assure immediate significance for
his efforts, his words and his deeds.

For different—and, indeed, frequently opposite
—reasons, these two social models were extremely
prestigious in the Palestinian Judaism of that
period. As we already know, a person could appropriate these models by being of levitical descent in
the first case, and, in the second, especially by
frequenting the teachers of the Pharisaic tradition.

In fact, he could boast either model or both
together. Zechariah, the father of the Precursor,
was a priest who belonged to the Abijah "class"
of the priesthood, and he had a wife, Elizabeth by
name, who was a descendant of Aaron. When came
the turn of Zechariah's "class" to serve, he would
perform his part of the Temple functions for a
week. Essentially, that is what was expected of him
according to the then current image of a dutiful
and pious priest: faithful participation in the liturgical service of the Temple of Jerusalem, and
scrupulous attention to "all the commandments
and observances of the Lord" (Lk. 1, 5-9). The
historian Flavius Josephus, a contemporary of
Jesus' first disciples, belonged, by birth, to one of

the greatest priestly families in the nation. Now, he himself has told us how, in his youth, he came to pledge his adherence to the Pharisaic school.[1] Saul of Tarsus belonged to the tribe of Benjamin. Having become a disciple of Jesus and then an apostle, Paul knew perfectly well, we can be sure, the effect he could still produce when—not without pride—he reminded his listeners that he had been trained in "the exact observance of the Law" at the feet of so famous and respected a teacher as Gamaliel.[2]

In the Palestinian Judaism of Jesus' time, therefore, being a "priest" or a "doctor of the Law," or both together, meant having an immediate and very solid social framework for one's activity. It

[1] Flavius Josephus, *Autobiography*, 2, 12. Concerning his priestly ancestry, he writes: "My family is not without glory, for it is sprung from priests. Different nations have different ways of determining nobility. In our nation, affinities with the priesthood are what make a family illustrious. Now, in my own case, not only is my family of sacerdotal descent, but it also belongs to the first of the twenty-four classes (already a considerable distinction) and, what is more, to the most illustrious of its tribes" (1, 1). Let us, if you wish, overlook Josephus' genealogical bragging. His words, at the very least, are a sufficiently faithful reflection of the distinction procured, in that milieu, by the social model of the levitical priesthood. In a manner of speaking, one's prestige doubled and one's social "presence" was consolidated proportionately if, in addition to being descended from the Levites, he was known to belong to the great Pharisaic tradition of legal interpretation.

[2] Acts 22, 3; Phil. 3, 5-6. See Acts 5, 34 concerning this same Gamaliel's intervention in behalf of Jesus' disciples: "One member of the Sanhedrin, however, a Pharisee called Gamaliel, who was a doctor of the Law and respected by the whole people, stood up . . ." Here again we see the influence of the social model on the milieu.

meant possessing, *from the start,* a first definition
of oneself in relation to one's milieu. It meant re-
ceiving a rich *heritage* of attitudes, accomplish-
ments and ways of doing whose significance, one
could be sure in advance, would, as a general rule,
be instantly grasped and accepted. In short, it
meant having a *presence* which had been previously
established, so to speak, by *titles that were recognized* and, in every respect, full of prestige.

Jesus Was Not a Priest

Now, as we know, Jesus did not possess any
of these titles at first. By birth, he belonged to
the tribe of Judah. His genealogy, as presented
by Matthew and Luke, even connects him, in a way,
with the house of David (Mt. 1, 1-17; Lk. 3, 23-38).
Hence, it could not occur to anyone in his family
to have him receive priestly training, for there
was absolutely nothing in their immediate entourage to warrant such an orientation. Correlatively, when he was old enough to shape his own
destiny, he did not think of himself or his activity
either, so far as we can know, in terms of the
levitical model. In his own eyes and in the eyes of
his family as well as his contemporaries, he was
approximately what we would call a "layman"
today. Therefore, from the standpoint of concrete
history where I am placing myself at this moment,
we should not view Jesus' presence among his
people as a priestly presence.

A Sacerdotalized Image of Jesus

Needless to say, such remarks take nothing
away from Jesus—nothing, at least, which really

belonged to him. Still, they may slightly alter the image we tend to form of him. Influenced, no doubt, by the weight of the models which obtrude themselves upon us today from the top to the bottom of the pastoral ladder, we unconsciously "sacerdotalize" almost everything about him—his outlook, his deeds, his methods, his utterance, his "mission," his program, his obedience, his fidelity, and even his inmost intentions, which we very often like to define by the concept of "sacrifice." We call him the "high priest" and the "priest" par excellence, and barely stop short of saying that he was *born* in order to *die* on the "altar" of the cross!

The Concept of "Ministry" in Relation to Jesus

This prefabricated and preaccepted image profoundly affects our views on the style of Jesus' activity and, as an immediate consequence, on the style of his presence among his people. Conscious or unconscious reference to this image is what causes us to go on speaking of Jesus' "ministry" as if that term were self-evidently right. Some are making a few scattered efforts to rectify both vocabulary and ideas in this connection, but the thinking of the Christian community as a whole —clergy included—is still far from being changed. For the most part, we cling to this idea of a "sacred ministry" by means of which we have for so long defined ourselves.

Early Christian Tradition Speaks of an "Activity"

We should observe, however, that the Gospel accounts give no indication of having ever considered the whole of Jesus' activity as a "ministry" in the sense attributed to that word especially since the third century.[3] As we have previously stated, they talk about "doing" and "saying." To be precise, then, it was what we today would call a "public activity." In this sense, the disciples of Emmaus could speak of "Jesus of Nazareth" as one "who proved he was a great *prophet* by the things he *said* and *did* in the sight of God and of the whole people" (Lk. 24, 19). That is the general image which contemporaries could form of Jesus' *activity* before his resurrection.

Mission and Service

Occasionally, it is true, Jesus himself, in referring to his "mission," spoke of his activity as a *service:* "The Son of Man himself did not come to be served but to serve, and to give his life as a ransom for many."[4] "To serve" translates the *ministrare* of our old Latin versions. But this *ministrare* does not, in itself, authorize our present notion of the "ministry" of Jesus—a notion derived, in point of fact, from the sacral world of the "priesthood."

Indeed, we need only consult the Greek to find that the *ministrare* in our Latin versions translates

[3] See what I have written on this subject in *Structures of Christian Priesthood: A study of home, marriage, and celibacy in the pastoral service of the Church* (New York: Macmillan, 1968), pp. 15-32 and 77-92.

[4] Mk. 10, 45. The same expression occurs in Mt. 20, 28, and in a still more telling form in Jn. 13, 2-15, which relates the washing of the disciples' feet during the Last Supper. In a spirit which is very close to John's and in the same context, there is also Lk. 22, 27.

diakonein, not *hierateuein,* not even *leitourgein* or any other verb of the same family.[5] Now, in the language of the Gospel narratives, *diakonein* generally connotes *domestic* "service" first of all, and, more specifically, "serving" *at table.*[6]

This is a far cry from the image of "service" in the Temple and at the altar, dimly alluded to by the popular notion of a "ministry" for Jesus. Compensatingly, we shall be much closer to the truth if we remember that Jesus, as someone entrusted with a "mission", was conscious of being engaged in a twofold service: on the one hand, the service of God, who had sent him, and, on the other, the service of his fellowmen, for whose benefit God's plan would start to be fulfilled.

Consequences for Our Pastoral Service

If I dwell on these distinctions, you can be sure it is not for the sole pleasure of procuring the academic advantages of precise terminology. On the contrary, it is because any distortion in our image of Jesus' presence among his people must, sooner or later, necessarily lead to a corresponding distortion in the *image of the presence of our pastoral service amid the Christian community itself.* In other words, any and all

[5] In Rom. 15, 16, Paul uses *hierourgein* to speak of his "ministering the Gospel" ["my priestly duty," in *The Jerusalem Bible*—Tr.]; but the context makes it clear that he is using the term metaphorically.

[6] Thus Mt. 8, 15; 25, 44; 27, 55; Mk. 15, 41; Lk. 4, 39; 8, 3; 10, 40; 17, 8; 22, 26-27. See Acts 6, 1-6 concerning the institution of the seven "deacons" in the community of Jerusalem. It will be noted, furthermore, that this kind of "service," as is natural, often devolves upon *women.*

views which more or less warp so decisive a model will inevitably warp, to the same degree, the suggestions that spring from it.

Specifically, visualizing Jesus' activity as a "ministry" means exposing ourselves to losing much of our sensitivity to his program and his options. It also means jeopardizing the legitimacy of *initiative and creativity* in our pastoral work, after having first dealt a blow to that same legitimacy in the ordinary conduct of our Christian life. As a general rule, a rigid model will produce only ready-made ideas and set behavior. In my opinion, one of the main obstacles to a profound renewal of the Christian community at this time comes from our long-since "sacerdotalized"—and, consequently, codified—image of Jesus' presence among his people. This is the image fostered among us by the prevalent idea of a "ministry" by Jesus.

The Viewpoint in the Epistle to the Hebrews

Moreover, let us not too hastily believe that this idea is endorsed by the Epistle to the Hebrews. The author knew too much about the Gospel event, on the one hand, and the structures of Judaism, on the other, to fall into such equivocation. In fact, his thinking explicitly presupposes that Jesus could not claim the status of the levitical priesthood as long as he remained among his people. He belonged, as the author observes, to "a different tribe, the members of which have never done service at the altar." Indeed, in the writer's estimation, it was common knowledge that Jesus "came from Judah, a tribe which Moses did not even mention when dealing with priests" (Heb. 7, 13-14). "In fact," he clearly asserts, *"if [Jesus] were on earth,* he would not be a priest (hiereus) at all, since there are others who make the offerings laid down by the Law" (8, 4).

But it is obvious that some Christians within earshot of the author were asking themselves questions. As Jews, they had known and loved the cultual pomp of the Temple of Jerusalem. This pomp had behind it the immense prestige of tradition and the Law: for centuries, it had been one of the vital forces in the history of Israel. Furthermore, some of these uneasy people perhaps belonged to the levitical priesthood by birth.

In any case, compared to that heritage, the Gospel event could appear *very modest.* Jesus came from Nazareth. He was descended from Judah—a fact which immediately barred him from the priesthood. More shocking yet, he had died nailed to a cross. Besides that, the distinctive structures of the Christian community seemed to offer nothing comparable to what was most reassuring and glorious in Judaism.[7] Should the Jews who had become Christians miss all those splendors? Should they feel *inferior* because of the cultual and sacral proximity of their erstwhile Judaism?

A Transhistoric Priesthood

That was the question, and it was extremely serious—all the more urgent since, beyond clear formulations, it touched profound sensibilities. In trying to answer it, the author did not do vio-

---

[7] On the internal organization of the early Christian community, see *Structures of Christian Priesthood,* pp. 93 ff.

lence to the reality of the Gospel event. Neither did he seek to involve the structures of the Christian community in a contest for the historical prestige attached to cultual and sacral splendor. For him, these things belonged to a bygone age.

His answer, therefore, springs directly from the realities of hope and faith. It is the answer, not of the letter, but of the spirit. Christians, he says in substance—and especially those who have come over from Judaism—need not anxiously eye the grandeurs of the priesthood of Aaron. They need not repeat or continue that episode, which, in truth, was only a "model" or a "reflection" of the things to come (8, 5; 10, 1). They need not seek easy assurances in a priestly and sacrificial structure like that which was established and protected by the Mosaic code.

For, although it is true that Jesus was not a "priest" *(hiereus)* of the same order as Aaron (7, 11), we must admit that he received an incomparably better "ministry" *(leiturgia: 8, 6)*, since, in his death and resurrection, he had access, not to the Holy of Holies, but to *God himself*. Now, it is in the presentation of this new "ministry" that the mysterious figure of Melchizedek enters. I would say that, in the overall line of reasoning, Melchizedek is the model that counterbalances the model of Aaron. Clearly then, the author continues, Jesus was not a "priest" *in time,* "of the order of Aaron," but *became* one, "beyond the veil" and *beyond history,* in eternity and for eternity—"a priest of the order of Melchizedek" (7, 11-28). To this new priesthood, which is "of a far higher order" than the old, there corresponds a new "covenant," which is also "better" than the old (8, 6-9, 28).

But, obviously, any further talk of "priesthood" mut henceforth refer to a *transhistoric* "priesthood" which properly belongs to the economy of hope and the order of the resurrection. In this sense, therefore, and in this sense alone, could the author still speak of Jesus as performing a "ministry" *(leitourgia)*. Accordingly, he refrained, as was fitting, from relating this idea to the beginnings of the Gospel event. He could not have done so, in fact, without flying in the face of historical reality —which is not the best way of accepting the "incarnation."

The Road Mapped Out for Us

In Christianity, we have to follow the road that has been thus mapped out. What we said earlier bears repetition: the ultimate meaning of the Gospel event should not, by a sharp turn, annul the more modest but necessary meaning of its beginnings. In this connection, furthermore, let us affirm that the style of Jesus' personal activity in no way suggests that we should introduce the levitical model into the pastoral service of the Christian community. In short, regardless of what we may have said and done in the past, the priesthood "of the order of Melchizedek"—which is a transhistoric, immutable and unique priesthood, exercised by Jesus "once and for all"—should not open the door to a new "levitism" among us, however well adapted it might seem. This would be tantamount to saying that we were in the process of transferring our hope, as the addressees of the

Epistle to the Hebrews seem to have been more or less unconsciously tempted to do.

Consequences for Jesus' Own Activity

These last remarks bring us back to Jesus' activity and to the beginnings of the Gospel event. Jesus was not a "priest" *(hiereus).* The style of his presence among his people was not, to begin with, of a sacerdotal turn. Because he did not belong to the tribe of Levi in the first place—not to mention many other factors, still more essential and decisive—Jesus does not seem to have modeled his program, his basic options, his utterance, his deeds or his methods on the sacrificial and sacral structure of the Palestinian Judaism of his day.[8] Strictly speaking, his activity was not a "ministry" *(leitourgia).* It was, if you will, a "service" *(diakonia);* but, in this sense, "service" was far from having the same specific character as "ministry." We shall, therefore, continue to speak simply of Jesus' "activity," since our meaning is now clear.

Jesus' Activity and That of the Precursor

From this point of view, it would be interesting to compare Jesus' activity and that of the Precursor. Both exhibited two very different styles of "prophetic" activity and utterance. Unfortunately, we know less about John's "instruction"

---

[8] In this connection, Jesus' attitude toward the Sabbath seems especially significant: Mt. 12, 1-8 and parallel passages; 12, 9-14 and par., etc. So, too, with regard to ablutions, Mt. 15, 1-9 and par.; the distinction between pure and impure, Mt. 15, 10-20 and par.; and sacrifice, Mt. 9, 10-13 and par.

(didakhe), although we know that he also had "disciples." Luke, among others, tells us in passing that John had taught his "disciples" a certain form of prayer (Lk. 11, 1; compare Mt. 9, 14 and par. with regard to fasting). Even more directly, it seems, do we glimpse the Precursor's type of "instruction" from Luke's general account of his utterance. In this account, "instruction" follows up "prophecy," as is natural.[9]

But what I want to call special attention to, right now, is the fact that John linked all his activity to a rite, one that was already familiar— a "baptism." From many viewpoints, this represented a decisive option. One result of it, in particular, was that the bulk of his activity was carried out in the vicinity of the Jordan. In this case, the rite, by its nature, imposed a severe limitation on the Precursor's freedom of movement. One had to go to the Jordan if one wanted to hear him and be baptized by him.

Without wishing to explain everything by this kind of observation, we can understand such an option fairly well if we remember that John was the son of the priest Zechariah. Far more than Jesus, the Precursor was a man dedicated to ritual and the Law. His personal heritage doubtlessly inclined him in that direction. Was it by chance that Jesus, on the other hand, refrained from immediately linking his word to a baptismal rite? No: another background and another heritage led to another style. The writer of the fourth Gospel

---

[9] See Lk. 3, 10-14, and notice the transition: "What must we do, then?"

expressly notes, in this respect, that, although a baptism was practiced among Jesus' disciples, *he himself*, however, *did not baptize* (Jn. 4, 1-3). At any rate, there is no doubt that this first abstention from ritual contributed much to the vast freedom of movement which he needed in the beginnings of the Gospel event.[10]

Jesus Had Not Been Schooled by the Legists

Excluded from the levitical priesthood by birth, Jesus had not attended the great schools conducted by the doctors of the Law, either. But we must not conclude therefrom that he knew nothing about the method and teaching of the "legists." The Gospel accounts prove the contrary.

Yet what struck Jesus' hearers was the *differences* rather than the similarities. The differences were such that many people, especially among the scribes and the Pharisees, were shocked. This marked the beginning of a conflict which soon grew more and more intense and ended in the crucifixion. As for Jesus' sympathizers and disciples, they declared with admiration that here was someone who did *not* teach "like the scribes." When they wanted to put it more precisely and positively, they emphasized the fact that he taught them "with authority" (Mt. 7, 29, and par.). This undoubtedly meant, first of all, that Jesus seemed to draw his teaching from inside himself, and, in addition, that he had something to say, if I may

10 Compare Paul's attitude: "Christ did not send me to baptize, but to preach the Good News" (1 Cor. 1, 17).

use that colloquialism. We can be sure, moreover, that this general characteristic, which applied to both style and content, was accompanied by many other "innovations."

Jesus and the Pharisees

Such remarks, needless to say, are not intended primarily to oppose Jesus to the Pharisees once more. Theology and pastoral zeal have often overworked this contrast, and not always in a very evangelical spirit, to say the least. Anything seemed legitimate in denigrating the Pharisees! To attain his true stature in Christian hope and faith, Jesus does not need to have us go about indulging in character assassination. What I wanted to highlight, rather, is, from a different angle, that astonishing *freedom of movement* which we have already seen so often in Jesus' activity. We are trying, at this moment, to form as exact an idea as possible of Jesus' presence among his people. That presence bore the stamp of a certain style. In order to go beyond the conventional images and grasp that style again, I deemed it useful to make passing mention of the initial *newness* of his "instruction."

All the same, it would be patently ridiculous to attribute this originality to the mere fact that Jesus had somehow or other escaped the mold of the traditional formation of the doctors of the Law. I do not intend to do so—especially since, in my view, this negative condition was compensated, in Jesus' case, by a very positive heritage, which he had been able to cull day after day in his little Galilean fatherland.

The Heritage of the "Brotherhood of the Poor"

I am referring here to the heritage of the "brotherhood of the poor." Unfortunately, we are rather ill-informed concerning the inner structures and life of this "brotherhood," whose widespread existence nevertheless shows through, here and there, in our documents.[11] But I think it altogether probable that this is where we should seek an important part of the immediate antecedents of the type of "instruction" which Jesus gave. Many clues point in this direction.[12] It is quite possible, therefore, that the originality and the freedom of manner which characterize Jesus' "instruction" were partly derived from the inspiration and the distinctive ways of the "brotherhood of the poor." Indeed, there is good reason to think that Jesus was born in this milieu and grew up in it. On the other hand, we are not saying much of anything definite—but, instead, are creating a goodly number of illusions— when we situate his birth, purely and simply, in the great totality of "Palestinian Judaism." For this was more diversified than we still too generally suppose.

[11] Although the critics have given but scant attention to this point, I firmly believe that our most accurate source of information on this "brotherhood of the poor" is found in the third "instruction" of the *Duae viae*, which, for this reason, I have called "The Instruction to the Poor." Those who are interested in studying the question further might consult my analysis of this text in *La Didachè, Instructions des apôtres* (Paris, 1958), pp. 308-347.

[12] In particular, Mt. 11, 28-30, not to mention the beatitudes themselves (Mt. 5, 3-10), which open the great collection of "instructions" known as the Sermon on the Mount (Mt. 5-7).

The Implementation and Progress of
Jesus' Evangelical Program

From the start, then, Jesus could not identify
either with the model of the "priest" or with that
of the "legist." But, at the same time, did not
the legacy of his people offer him other paths,
much broader, much freer and, especially, much
more open to new creations?

Jesus Had Come, Not To Repeat, But To Create

Jesus had come, not to repeat, but to create.
In his mind, the evangelical program was a "new
wine" it would have been unwise to put into "old
wineskins" (Mt. 9, 17). Somewhat later, it seems,
at a moment we cannot determine with certitude,
the Gospel event was expressly referred to as the
"Good News." In every way, this expression ade-
quately translated the profound purpose and the
essential significance of Jesus' "mission." On the
one hand, it underlined the "freshness" of it and,
on the other, clearly implied a renewal of "hope."

Ties with the Past

Now, in any activity which describes the principal axis of a great destiny, *the newness itself must
take on an accessible and receivable form* in the
milieu in which it occurs. This is a law of history,
which recognizes no such thing as an absolute
beginning. A certain organic tie with the past
is a necessity common to all our undertakings,
however original we may imagine they are and

however decisive we may wish them to be. The whole thing, then, is evidently knowing how to *choose,* from the heritage of the past, those fecund ties which still hold serious promise for the future.

Jesus did not escape these general conditions of any activity which is genuinely integrated into the unbreakable continuity of human time. The only way to escape them would have been to discard the global perspective of the "incarnation." In order to offer his people precisely what was newest about his message, Jesus had to choose the efficacious models of his activity from the heritage of the past. And it is surely in connection with these models that he gradually had to make some of the crucial *options* of his life.

The Twofold Model of Prophet and Sage

We actually know the result of that process. Above the current models of the "priest" and the "doctor of the Law," there were yet the two ancient models of the "prophet" and the "sage." Both still enjoyed enormous prestige, though in different degrees. Each, in its own fashion, was an *open* model and, therefore, was already capable of introducing into the consciousness of Israel a large part of what was newest in all that the Gospel event would create. In the first stage, at the very least, the seed of a truly new hope could be planted starting from there.

Transcending These Models

The two models of the "prophet" and the "sage" were likewise open in the sense that they both allowed of being *surpassed* at the opportune moment. Thus it is that Jesus could one day imply that his activity brought something better than the "prophets" and saints of old had ever seen.[13] Similarly, he could declare, on another occasion, that there was in him "something greater than Solomon," the traditional prototype of "sages" (Mt. 12, 42 and par.).

The Titles "Christ" and "Lord"

At a pivotal point in Jesus' activity, the properly messianic title of "the Anointed" *(khristos)* presented itself as a transcending of the initial prophetic model. This is a fact which we must never forget if we are to appreciate his messianism and, in a special way, his title of "king" (Mt. 21, 1-11 and par.; also Jn. 18, 33-37).

One day, then, as he was walking with his disciples along the road to Caesarea Philippi, Jesus asked them, "Who do people say I am?" They replied, "John the Baptist; others, Elijah; others again, one of the prophets." He continued, "But you, who do you say I am?" Peter answered, "You are the Christ." Then Jesus ordered them not to talk to anyone about him under that name (Mk. 8, 27-30 and par.). Later—and especially on his triumphal entry into Jerusalem—the messianic title was to be still more widely used, while wait-

---

[13] Especially Mt. 11, 11-13; 12, 41 ("there is something *greater* than Jonah here"); 13, 16-17; Lk. 10, 23-24; 16, 16. In the very significant scene of the transfiguration, the disciples see their master conversing familiarly with Moses and Elijah (Mt. 17, 3 and par.). Compare, in a kindred sense, Jesus' evaluation of the Precursor: "What did you go out into the wilderness to see? [...] A prophet? Yes, I tell you, and *much more than a prophet*" (Lk. 7, 26; Mt. 11, 9).

ing for the resurrection to crown this whole
development with the title of "Lord" or "Son of
God."

The Development of Jesus' Activity

Prophet and teacher, then prophet and sage
superior to the greatest names of the past, then
messiah and king, Lord and Son of God—the
successive acquisition of these titles marks a definite progression of *meaning* in Jesus' activity. At
the same time, it outlines the essential unfolding
of the Gospel event. In all this, naturally, there
were slowdowns and delays; but, as we well know,
there were also sudden gains and dazzling con-
quests. The Gospel event did not develop in a
straight line. It encountered much resistance, which
Jesus sometimes had to overcome and sometimes
circumvent.[14] The business at hand was, first, to
mix the yeast in with the dough; the dough could
rise only with time (Mt. 13, 33; Lk. 13, 20-21).
But, despite obstacles and circuity, Jesus' titles progressively and vigorously defined the style and
significance of his presence among his people. The
ultimate meaning carried hope beyond history.
As Lord, or Son of God, Jesus became the "initia-
tor of life" for all those who would accept the gift
of it through faith (Acts 3, 15; 5, 31).

The Initial Message and the Prophetic Model

Let us not, however, neglect the starting point.

[14] It is significant that this resistance occurred even in
Jesus' immediate milieu. One day, as Mark relates, his own
relatives "set out to take charge of him, convinced he was
out of his mind" (Mk. 3, 21; compare Jn. 7, 5).

Jesus was—so everyone thought—the son of Joseph, a carpenter in Nazareth. Could "anything good" come from that little town lost in the Galilean "melting pot" (Jn. 1, 46)? After his baptism in the waters of the Jordan and a brief sojourn in the desert, Jesus' first act, with a view to fulfilling his "mission," was to appropriate the ancient model of the prophet, Yahweh's messenger.[15] In keeping with this model—which, incidentally, was only an adaptation of the social type of the

---

[15] Lk. 4, 18-19, quoting Is. 61, 1-2. Notice that Luke, unlike Mk. 6, 1-6 and Mt. 13, 53-58, places this episode at the beginning of Jesus' activity. For the narrator, the reading of Is. 61, 1-2 in the synagogue at Nazareth evidently took on an exemplary and polyvalent value:

> The spirit of the Lord has been given to me,
> for he has anointed me.
> He has sent me [that is, given me a mission]
> to bring the good news to the poor,
> to proclaim liberty to captives
> and to the blind new sight,
> to set the downtrodden free,
> to proclaim the Lord's year of favor.

Let us observe in passing that we must not press this text unduly and conclude from it, as some do, that Jesus addressed himself to the "poor" first of all. How could he have done so? The style of his activity, patterned at this time on the herald's, led him, on the contrary, to deliver his message to the *entire population of Galilee*. That is why he began by going "round the whole of Galilee" (Mt. 4, 23; Mk. 1, 39; Lk. 4, 14-15). The expression in Is. 61, 1—"He has sent me to bring good news to the poor"—should be understood, not in a restrictive, but in a global sense. Restricting Jesus' initial *message* to the poor and the outcasts of fortune is a contradiction in terms. What is true, on the other hand, is that the *signs,* by their very nature, were obviously meant to touch, first of all, those who were in *need:* the deaf, the blind, the lame, the infirm and the afflicted of all kinds. The altogether special attention which Jesus paid to their distress testified, precisely, to the universality of his message and of the hope which it brought.

herald—Jesus *swiftly* bore this "message" *(kerugma)* from God through the cities, towns and villages of Galilee: "The time has come, and the kingdom of God is close at hand. Repent, and believe the Good News" (Mk. 1, 15). There, in practically the same words, no doubt, was the initial message of Jesus in his role as prophet.

The Message Is Not a Discourse

There, too, we can see the extremely vital and supple style of this first period. Some, it seems, are not particularly fond of dwelling on these beginnings: you would think the image disquiets them. As far as they are concerned, it is understood that everything began with a long "discourse," which is obviously the Sermon on the Mount (Mt. 5-7). An "inaugural speech," defined as the "charter" of the kingdom of God and the proclamation of the "new law"—this, they feel, evidences far more seriousness and better organization. Let us add that it is also more reassuring. The meager prophetic utterance which we are bidden to take as the starting point of such a vast upheaval, is really too slight, they believe, and—especially—much too fluid. It must necessarily be another of those engines of war set up by disrespectful and rather inconsiderate persons who want to shake the "institution."

There, that is what really bothers them! What shall we answer? Three things. First, no one can change history as he likes. Now, because our accounts report the facts clearly enough, it is certain, in my opinion, that Jesus inaugurated his activity with a very brief "message," which he swiftly carried throughout the whole of Galilee.[16]

On the other hand, it is just as certain regardless of what has been said, that the Sermon on the Mount was not *delivered* in the manner of an "inaugural speech" before an attentive audience which miraculously registered, for the generations yet to come, all the clauses of a "new law." The reason is very simple: the Sermon on the Mount is *not a discourse, but a collection of short "instructions" (didakhai)*, scrupulously transmitted as such from *teacher* to *disciples*, on *many* occasions, for the most part lost today.[17] Furthermore, the mention of a "charter" or "law" in connection with this anthology of "instructions" sends our reading off on the wrong track. Unless we wish to go astray here, we must keep a very close watch over our instruments of analysis. On Jesus' lips, an "instruction" was ordinarily not a "precept"— and still less a "legal" disposition.

Lastly, in a civilization where heralds were

---

[16] Here, the fundamental testimony remains that of Mk. 1, 14-15. It is in the light of this that we must read Mt. 4, 17 and Lk. 4, 14, among other texts. Against this background, there then stands out the general account in Mt. 4, 23-25 (Compare Lk. 4, 15-30). We notice, moreover, that the first "mission" of the Twelve seems to have taken on a style identical with that of Jesus' initial "message," as is only natural. Consequently, we can judge one by the other (Mt. 10, 1-6 and par.).

[17] Regarding this idea of an "inaugural speech," we should note that the equivalent of the Sermon on the Mount from Matthew is placed considerably later in Luke's narrative (6, 20-49). In addition, the "Our Father," which was certainly transmitted in the manner of an "instruction," furnishes an excellent test: Matthew has incorporated it into the Sermon on the Mount (6, 9-13), whereas Luke has linked it to a more specific circumstance (11, 1-4).

almost as familiar as newspapers, radio and tele-
vision are to us today, a "message" like that of
Jesus—such as we read it in Mk. 1, 15—rested,
sociologically, on one of the most living and best
accepted forms of public speaking. What we should
retain from it, therefore, in our present perspective, is not the image of a prophet who wantonly
defies all the rules for well-thought-out activity,
but, on the contrary, that of a man who judici-
ously *chooses* his means *with regard for the concrete conditions of his milieu and his era.* Still,
this example of realism and solid reason may
carry implications for our own ecclesial situation.
We shall always stand to gain if we go along with
life instead of trying to preserve outworn gestures,
customs and institutions at any cost. In his options, Jesus gave proof of more wisdom and liberty.

The Length of the First Galilean Tour

How long was that first Galilean tour? Several weeks at the very least, but most likely a
few months.[18] Regardless of the exact chronology,

---

[18] Note, in this connection and for this period, the al-
lusions to habitual "teaching" by Jesus in the synagogues
during the *Sabbath* assemblies: "He *went round the whole of
Galilee* teaching *(didaskon)* in their synagogues, proclaiming
(kerusson) the Good News of the kingdom..." (Mt. 4, 23;
Mk. 1, 39; Lk. 4, 15). As he went along, Jesus apparently
used these assemblies to *announce* his "mission," in the style
of the incident at Nazareth as related by Luke. Luke must
have judged that this episode was well suited to illustrate the
kind of "teaching" which Jesus practiced during the period
when he was principally occupied with spreading the "Good
News" of the coming of the kingdom of God throughout
Galilee (Lk. 4, 14-15). After having read Is. 61, 1-2:
The Spirit of the Lord has been given to me....

it is important to preserve the particular character of this initial period. Otherwise, we are in great danger of hopelessly muddling two essential aspects of Jesus' activity and thereby confusing the concrete modalities according to which he chose, at the start, to guarantee himself an efficacious presence among his people.

The Herald's Mode of Activity

The herald *(kerux)* had an absolutely distinctive mode of activity; and, as a consequence, he also had a manner of living which flowed partly from the necessities of that same activity. The symbols of his function were a voice and a foot.[19]

He has sent me to bring the good news to the poor. . . .
to proclaim the Lord's year of favor,

Jesus rolled up the scroll, returned it to the assistant, sat down and declared in substance, "This text is being fulfilled today even as you listen" (Lk. 4, 16-21). We must not, as is usually done, confuse this early synagogal "teaching" with that which Jesus later transmitted to his *disciples* in his capacity as *teacher*. For the moment, he was still primarily the *herald* who presented himself before his people on the part of God, like the ancient prophets, and who revealed the essence of his "mission" at the same time as he began to accomplish it.

[19] Is. 40, 3:
A *voice* cries, "Prepare in the wilderness . . ."
and 52, 7:
How beautiful on the mountains
are the *feet* of one who brings good news,
who heralds peace, brings happiness,
proclaims salvation,
and tells Zion,
"Your God is king!"

This last text is partially quoted in Rom. 10, 15, precisely in regard to the "mission" of an apostle, the messenger of the Gospel. In addition, note this explicit reference to the same symbol when Paul discusses the participation of *Christians*

The herald is a "voice" in the service of the person who has sent him: that is the essence of his function. He should possess a clear, strong voice, for he cries out even more than he speaks. Not a maker of long discourses, he is a man who announces and proclaims. His glory consists in being found faithful. He is alert and mobile, with the road as the proper place and instrument of his "service" *(diakonia)*. For that reason, he should ordinarily still be young. One of the chief qualities of his service is promptness. He must be ready to go at any moment: as soon as he receives the call, he must be disposed to leave everything—home, father and mother, brothers and sisters, wife and children. In this sense, he must be free, so as to carry out his mission posthaste.[20] The simplicity of his costume is also symbolic of his function and of the style of life which accompanies it. A certain despoilment is the normal condition of a herald's life. In every respect, his glory lies in being able to say that he went to the very end of his "course" *(dromos)*.[21]

---

in disseminating the Gospel: "[Wear] for *shoes* on your *feet* the *eagerness* to spread the gospel of peace" (Eph. 6, 15) .

[20] It is obviously with this social model of the herald in mind that we must, in part, understand Jesus' injunctions to his "disciples" when he "sent" them for the first time to bear the "Good News" from city to city, from village to village and from house to house (Mk. 6, 7-13; Mt. 10, 1-16; Lk. 9, 1-6 and 10, 1-16) . We would be misinterpreting these injunctions if we took them *primarily* as permanent exigencies of "poverty." They are, first of all, conditions of service in a certain style of activity defined by the model of the herald.

[21] Compare Paul's sentiments in Acts 20, 24: "But life to me is not a thing to waste words on, provided that when

The Purpose of This First Phase

For some time at the beginning of his public activity, therefore, Jesus deliberately leaned on the ancient model of the prophet, Yahweh's herald. Very close by, John had first exemplified a similar renewal of ancient prophecy: "In the fifteenth year of Tiberius Caesar's reign . . . the word of God came to John, son of Zechariah, in the wilderness" (Lk. 3, 1-2). During these first months, Jesus speedily spread, throughout Galilee, a message that was terse but charged with meaning and consequences and impact. From this brief message, the *Gospel* event itself would eventually draw its name (Mk. 1, 1.14-15). Jesus apparently felt that, before anything else, he had singlehandedly to break through the very center of his people's consciousness. Thanks to that *first breach,* successive blows would gradually enable the fullness of a new and decisive hope to enter in.

Message and Instruction

I have often discussed these things; but because I have a nagging suspicion that we experience much difficulty appreciating them today in all the power and authenticity of their origins, I have allowed myself to dwell on them once more.

I finish my race [*ton dromon mou*] I have carried out the mission [*ten diakonian:* literally, the service] the Lord Jesus gave me—and that was to bear witness to the Good News [*to euaggelion*] of God's grace [goodwill, favor, love]"; also in 13, 25: "Before John ended his career [*ton dromon*]," speaking of the Baptist, whom Paul portrays as messenger and herald; or in 2 Tim. 4, 7: "I have fought the good fight to the end; I have run the race [*ton dromon*] to the finish."

As a matter of fact, when we now speak of Jesus' "message," or the "Gospel message," we usually drown the "message" in the sea of "instruction." To that extent, the *prophet* whom Jesus wanted *primarily* to be, is submerged under the more familiar features of the *teacher*.

Then we wonder why we have trouble understanding. Actually, it is we who have more or less confused everything to begin with, by indiscriminately mixing models, deeds, methods, attitudes, activity and utterance. And, indeed, it must be admitted that, *from a literary viewpoint,* our Gospel narratives give far more place to Jesus' instruction than to his message. Among many other examples, we need only take the Sermon on the Mount and the parables, all of which belong to the literary form known as "instruction."

But this literary equilibrium is perfectly natural, since the message, though *frequently repeated,* did not constitute a real *discourse* or, still less, a *series of discourses* more or less connected by their form and purpose. As incorporated into Jesus' activity, the message had to remain brief. Instruction, on the contrary, called for *variety and development.* Still, we must not be misled by appearances: for, despite the brief literary space it occupies, the *message* is what gives the instruction its *basic* and *ultimate* meaning, just as, *in the first place,* it is what diffuses through the entire Gospel event its fundamental quality of "Good News."

The Instruction Completes the Message

Still, having been introduced thus into the consciousness of chance listeners, the "message" *(kerugma)* had limitations which Jesus, more than anyone, could not overlook. In the order of action, the "message" required a complement, and that complement had to be of a different nature. It took the form of the "instruction" *(didakhe),* which we have already mentioned several times.

Jesus Takes On Disciples and Becomes a Teacher

At a certain moment—probably after a long journey through Galilee—Jesus therefore made an important decision: he would take on "disciples" (Mk. 1, 16-20 and par.). To the role of "prophet," which was already acknowledged as his, he thus added that of "teacher" *(didaskalos;* Luke uses *epistates* six times). Now, for Jesus, becoming a "teacher" meant, in the first place, giving a new form to his utterance. But, right from the start, it also meant accepting a proportionate modification in the *rhythm* and *style* of his activity, not to mention many other consequences which affected his very way of living.

Teacher and herald: these two titles designated models of activity which were quite different from one another—so different, in fact, that we can hardly think of them as blended together and utilized simultaneously. But then the accounts by Matthew, Mark and Luke suggest no such fusion; instead, what they constantly imply is *alternation.* After a first breakthrough—that of the initial "message"—Jesus paused, surrounded himself with "disciples," adopted the social behavior and literary practices of a "teacher," and thus dedicated himself to what was then called "instruction."

The Teacher's Mode of Activity

What does this mean? In the Palestinian milieu of that period, giving an "instruction" to "disciples," on the part of a "teacher" like Jesus, did not in any way mean delivering a "speech" in one continuous stream, as the lecturers and orators of the Greco-Roman world could then do. We would be totally mistaken if we imagined, for instance, that Jesus' parables, which are so characteristic of his "instruction," were simply "spoken" like a discourse, and that the disciples had nothing better to do afterwards than piece together their precious accounts from the fragmentary recollections which a flowing delivery might have fixed in their memory.

In point of fact, an instruction presupposes that the teacher has carefully chosen his subject beforehand, mapped out its development and, often, determined the precise wording in his mind. By the time he speaks, therefore, his instruction generally possesses a definite form. The master sits down, surrounded by his disciples, who, as a rule, are not very numerous. By its nature, an instruction is not meant for large crowds. Assuredly, the "crowds" may be there, as our accounts often state (partly, no doubt, to show the favor which he enjoys). But, even in the presence of "crowds"—whose numerical importance should not be exaggerated, since we read of a "crowd" in an ordinary house (Mk. 3, 32)—the teacher is, in general, primarily seeking the attention of his closest disciples, in the twofold meaning of the word.

Strictly speaking, they are the ones to whom he transmits his "instruction."

This he does by *repeating* his dicta until they are lodged in the minds of his disciples. Once this first memorizing has been accomplished, there follows, if need be, a period of explanation in the form of questions and answers (thus Mk. 4, 13-20 and par.). The teacher thus makes sure that his instruction has been not only retained but understood. In short, the instruction is a genuine "teaching" *(didaskein)*, in the style of the times and the milieu; and, if properly received, it leads to a measure of "understanding" and "knowledge" *(eidenai, ginoskein)*.

Every feature of Jesus' instruction, therefore, sharply distinguishes it from the type of discourse which aims primarily at mere persuasion. Consequently, in order to understand how the parables, or the short instructions collected in the Sermon on the Mount, have reached us in their present state, we need not imagine that Jesus' first hearers were endowed with a miraculous memory or that the evangelical tradition performed feats of reconstructing the past. It suffices that Jesus was an admirably gifted "teacher" in his line—which he was; and it suffices that his most faithful listeners were real "disciples"—which they were also.

But what a difference, then, when we compare his instruction and his message! His message went out to chance listeners, whereas his instruction was addressed, before all, to disciples who followed their teacher wherever he went. His message made provision for constant and quick-paced traveling, whereas his instruction, without tying him down like a school teacher, obliged him to decelerate the rhythm of his activity considerably.

As a Teacher, Jesus Remains Relatively Mobile

Having become a "teacher," and being recognized as such, Jesus therefore remained relatively mobile. In order to be his "disciple," one had to be ready to "follow" him, in the original and strict sense of the word. But there was an enormous difference between this relative mobility and the accelerated itinerancy of the "prophet," the herald of the "Good News." It seems, moreover, that after a period of more intensive instruction, during which he took special care of his disciples, and particularly the Twelve, Jesus returned, on various occasions, to the essential activity that marked the beginnings of the Gospel event. From all indications, he did so, in particular, during the first "mission" of the disciples themselves (Mt. 11, 1; comp. Lk. 8, 1).

The Subordination of Instruction to Message

These differences, however, should not be exaggerated. For Jesus' instruction, though *subordinated* to his message, was at the same time *coordinated* with it, as we can see especially in the parables of the kingdom. The breach which his message had brusquely made in the hope of the Galileans would be slowly and patiently enlarged by his instruction, so as to afford eventual passage to the fullness of the "Good News." Although no text allows us to judge of this apodictically, such, it seems, was Jesus' intention when, at the end of his first Galilean journey, he surrounded himself with "disciples"

and cast his utterance in the form of "instructions."
The teacher's intention is here stamped on the
facts, and this clue is enough for us.[22]

If, after that, we consider the general plan
of his activity and, therefore, the style of his presence among his people, we shall have to conclude
that Jesus wanted to be, first and foremost, the
"herald" of the "Good News" of the "kingdom of
God." Consequently, his "instruction" in his capacity as "teacher," however extensive, we subordinate
to his "message." With regard to that message,
Jesus' activity drew its inspiration—though very
freely, of course—from the model offered by the
ancient *prophets,* especially those who had presented themselves to the people as Yahweh's heralds, or messengers.

Jesus' Instruction and Its Models:
The Tradition of the Sages

As for his instruction, it seems mainly to have
followed the model set forth by the *sages* of the
past—a model which had already been partly renewed, besides, under the more recent influence of
the ideal embodied by the "scribes." These men
were dedicated to preserving and exploiting the
precious treasure of Israel's heritage which the
"scriptures" had become: whence their name of
"scribes" and also, from one point of view, the
particular style of their "wisdom."[23] This current

[22] For these last paragraphs, I have drawn extensively on
what I have written elsewhere about Jesus' "instruction."
See *Structures of Christian Priesthood,* pp. 22-24.

[23] We again find the same prophet-sage-scribe association
in connection with Jesus' disciples: "I am sending you

—which, furthermore, the "brotherhood of the poor" drew upon in an original way—is doubtlessly where we should situate Jesus' "instruction." In any case, it would be paradoxical to align his "instruction," more or less implicitly, on the distinctive orientations and practices or the Pharisaic tradition.

The Title of "Son of Man" in the Framework of Jesus' Activity

Furthermore, in my opinion, the general framework of Jesus' *activity* is what enables us to understand most advantageously a title about which we have not yet spoken: that of "Son of Man" (Mt. 8, 20, etc.). This title has given rise to diverse interpretations. Some have tried to shed light on it from its literary origins (especially Dan. 7, 13). Without denying the value of such comparisons, we would observe, however, that this method tends more or less to overlook the *global reason* why Jesus *chose* to present himself under this title many times. Beyond question, it reflected a well-thought-out option on his part. Now, to what did it correspond?

Personally, placing myself anew in the perspec-

---

prophets and wise men and scribes" (Mt. 23, 34; comp. Lk. 11, 49, where the substitution of "apostles" for "sages" and "scribes" should probably be considered a secondary adaptation, attributable either to the narrator himself or to the early Christian community. Note, on the other hand, in the immediate context, the explicit mention of the "Wisdom of God"). The popular reaction to Jesus' "instruction" is interesting from our present viewpoint: "Where did the man get this *wisdom* and these miraculous powers? This is the carpenter's son, surely?" (Mt. 13, 54-55). Again, concerning the formation of the ideal of the "scribes" in the traditional current of wisdom, we may read, in particular, Ecclus. 24, 1-34 and 39, 1-11.

tive of the concrete necessities of Jesus' *activity,* I
would say that he appropriated this title in somewhat the same way as the ancient prophets chose
to present themselves—and their *message* at the
same time—in the light of formulas like "Oracle of
Yahweh" or "Thus says the Lord of hosts." Such
formulas rested implicitly on the social model of
the herald. They defined a double relationship: to
God and to the people. Thus, they situated prophetic activity as a "mission," of which they became the proper *sign* and *instrument.*

By situational analogy, the title of "Son of Man"
would be very well understood along these lines.
Jesus had chosen to base himself on the model of
the prophet at first. But he was *more* than a prophet, and he knew it (Mt. 12, 41, etc.). Therefore,
he could not be content with saying, for example,
in order to situate his activity, "Thus says Yahweh,
the God of Israel" or something similar. Because of
their earlier use, all such formulas had become
closed formulas. Jesus was to *transcend* prophecy,
so as to situate himself in the messianic line when
the time came. Therefore, he needed an *open* formula.

*Utilizing the Title of "Son of Man" as an
Instrument of Activity*

The title of "Son of Man," which Jesus used
on many occasions, possessed this very advantage:
it had a fluid and polyvalent meaning. Neither too
precise nor too vague, it remained *open* to all the
meanings which the Gospel event would progressively reveal. In short, in the unique situation in
which Jesus found himself with regard to God as

well as those to whom God had sent him, the title of "Son of Man" represented an *excellent instrument of activity.*

Thanks largely to a very skillful use of this instrument furnished by the prophetic heritage of the past, Jesus was able, at least in the beginning, to make both the true quality of his *person* and the ultimate meaning of his *mission* understood and gradually accepted. Indeed, the title of "Son of Man" fit Jesus' *personal activity* so well that, after the resurrection, it rapidly fell out of use in the first Christian communities.[24] Having served its purpose, it could disappear and make way for the new acquisitions which it had definitively secured. For the "new wine" there was now need of "new skins."

The Great Objective: A Decisive Renewal of Hope for All Men

But an activity is not defined only by its conditions, its options and its means: it is defined still more by its goal. Therefore, I would like to complete this analysis of the various elements in Jesus' presence among his people by briefly examining its objective.

The Global Aim of the Gospel Event

To tell the truth, the essence of what I shall try to shed light on here, is already implicitly con-

[24] Apart from the Gospels, it is used only in Acts 7, 56 and Rev. 1, 13 and 14, 14.

tained in the initial message. May I be forgiven
for bringing it up once more, as I quote Mark:
"The time has come, and the kingdom of God
is close at hand. Repent, and believe the Good
News" (1, 15).

In order to define the global aim of the Gospel
event, we commonly say that Jesus came to "bring"
us salvation, or the hope of salvation, on the part
of God. Frankly, I am less and less drawn to the
idea of someone's "bringing" us hope. It is too rem-
iniscent of the *passive* incarnation which we discussed earlier. Is Jesus merely someone who
"brought" us, if I may use the expression, a ready-
made hope?

Creating a Decisive Hope for All Men

The Gospels, at any rate, focusing unanimously
and consistently on the many labors entailed in a
large-scale *activity,* suggest something entirely different. In fact, we shall translate the reality of the
Gospel event much better if we say that Jesus came
to *create* among his people a decisive hope which
was destined to reach all men ultimately. In Jesus'
hands, hope was not something established from
the start, but something to be *constructed* during
the whole of an admirable and perilous enterprise.
It was a *task* unevenly distributed over each stage
along the road, rather than a gift to be delivered,
intact, to the addressee. In brief, evangelical hope
was like the seed which prepares a huge tree, or
like the yeast which gradually raises all the dough
(Mt. 13, 31-33). Besides, it was really God himself
who created that hope in the activity and person
of Jesus.[25]

Such, then, was the essential aim of the Gospel program: by a total renewal of ancient hope, *to create a decisive hope,* destined to reach one and all eventually, by paths as diverse as the concrete conditions of man's individual and collective pilgrimage through time. Despite appearances, no one was excluded—neither in the past nor in the present nor in the future. This was a universal hope. Otherwise, everything was meaningless, both in the heart of man and in the very program of God.

The Announcement of the Kingdom of God Gives Us an Inkling of That Hope

To give man an inkling of these things, Jesus used a simple means, perhaps, but one that proved effective in the general atmosphere of that period and milieu. I am referring to an image: that of the "kingdom of God." This image, we must admit, has aged a great deal. How many of us still feel its power and grasp its implications? When certain people talk about the "kingdom of God," they sound as if they are awaiting some ideal organization of virtue through the concerted efforts of obedience and law.

The Significance of the Image of the Kingdom

Let us simply say that that is not the point. Moreover, Jesus did not invent this figure. It already existed equivalently in the ancient tradition.[26] It had even become familiar to the Judaism of

[25] Jn. 5, 17: "My Father goes on working, and so do I."
[26] Thus, for example, in Is. 52, 7, which we have already quoted in another connection:

Jesus' day—with variable meanings, however, where the present or the future, particularism or universalism, the merit of obedience to law or a free gift were in the forefront, according to circumstances and basic intellectual orientations.

In any case, the idea of a "kingdom of God" always contained a more or less explicit avowal of the *failure of the royalty of man*. History had seen so many kings mount their thrones, so many dynasties and empires and political systems of all kinds, which, after having held forth the promise of renewed hope, had all unfailingly collapsed, sooner or later, amid countless disappointments.

What could one now expect from such systems? Having been let down by man, Israel—starting especially from the exile—gradually and increasingly transferred its expectation to a *royalty of God himself,* exercised in the midst of his people, as was often thought, by one to whom he would give that power: the mysterious "Anointed," or the "King" par excellence, the "Messiah," the new David. The idea of a "kingdom of God" thus became like a *motor image,* somehow linked to the present and the past by virtue of covenants and promises, but especially projected onto the future, on the indeterminate horizon of history. By that very fact, the "kingdom of God" appeared as a

---

How beautiful on the mountains
are the feet of one who brings good news,
who heralds peace, brings happiness,
proclaims salvation,
and tells Zion,
"Your God is king!"

Note, however, that this text refers to Yahweh's royalty over Israel (thus, expressly, 1 Chr. 28,5).

maximal image, in which, so to speak, the *totality of human hope* was concentrated.

From Hope in the Kingdom to Hope in Life

Jesus' initial message proclaimed, from God, the imminent manifestation of this "kingdom"; "The time has come, and the kingdom of God is close at hand. Repent, and believe the Good News" (Mk. 1, 15). We can imagine the stir produced by such an announcement. On the lips of this herald, in whom the people soon discerned a "prophet" such as had never been seen before, and then on the lips of this "teacher," who progressively unveiled God's plan in the familiarity of the "instruction," the "kingdom of God" was essentially, from the beginning to the end of the Gospel event, the image of a *totality of hope.*

The abundant "signs" which accompanied his message and his instruction also carried the very same implication: "If it is through the Spirit of God that I cast devils out, then know that the kingdom of God has overtaken you."[27] With time, Jesus was recognized, and then acclaimed, as "messiah." And finally, when the consternation caused by his tragic and ignominious death had been dispelled, his resurrection showed that the hope of the "kingdom" was nothing less, in a word, than the *hope*

[27] Mt. 12, 28 and par. In the same vein is Jesus' reply to John's disciples: "Go back and tell John what you hear and see; the blind see again, and the lame walk, lepers are cleansed, and the deaf hear, and the dead are raised to life and the Good News is proclaimed to the poor; and happy is the man who does not lose faith in me" (Mt. 11, 4-6 and par.) .

of a new life with God himself, which was later called "eternal life" or "life" pure and simple (Jn. 20, 31; 1 Jn. 1, 1-4).

A Last Look at Jesus' Evangelical Program

That is how Jesus' evangelical program, starting from the "Good News" of the "kingdom of God," progressed toward the creation of a new hope. Here was the goal toward which everything converged. As we have often had occasion to observe, the heritage of Israel's long past was widely utilized in the implementation of his program. But it was always utilized in a new way. Jesus' activity certainly did not set us the example of cozy tradition that remains withdrawn inside itself. When he had to choose, he simply abandoned the paths which were too cluttered for those which were wide open. At one and the same time realistic, respectful and free, his activity contained no fetishism on the one hand and no anarchy on the other, but only supreme daring and lucidity. Thus it was that over the ancient land of the chroniclers, prophets and sages, the Gospel event burst forth like a new springtime.

There Remains Much Hope To Be Created: Our Pastoral and Christian Programs

Have we gone into another season? That is not what Jesus expected of us. The Church's pastoral program, like the Christian program itself, is, at bottom, only an *appropriation* of the Gospel program, variable according to the circumstances of history—individual and collective—and yet consistent with what existed in the beginning. Repetition does not guarantee fidelity. Like Jesus, we need freedom in order to be faithful. Laws are good, they are necessary; but they should not put a stranglehold on choice. Why are we fearful? Has the Spirit of God turned into an obsession about the risks inherent in life and liberty?

We still have much hope to create if we want to be faithful to the Gospel. Loving is difficult, but hoping is perhaps even more so. The seed of hope, like that of love, lies in desire and joy; and it dies if deprived of this rich soil. But sometimes, after the first germination, hoping also means questioning and combating. Jesus did not evade this sort of confrontation which so often obstructed his path. We need the hope that perdures through periods of elation and of difficulty. At day's end, we shall be asked only one thing: to have been good builders of the hope of "life."

II
Jesus in the
Early Christian Community

There is still quite a bit of confusion about the birth of the first Christian communities. In general, we are inclined to attribute the whole work of organization to Jesus himself. At times, we barely stop short of turning his habitual audiences into "liturgical assemblies" or looking upon the Twelve, in particular, as forming a veritable "community" right from the start. For centuries, it was even thought possible to discern in Jesus' entourage all the essential features of monasticism, which, in turn, has done so much to shape the life of those who are chiefly entrusted with the pastoral service of the Christian community. It is sufficiently evident, furthermore, that this kind of thinking still obsesses many of us. Need we add, however, that it proceeds too fast and, especially, much too far? For this reason, I would like to start by clarifying the situation a little with what I believe is a more exact analysis of our earliest documents.

Once that point has been cleared up, I shall try to describe, from various viewpoints, the general equilibrium of values on which the early Christian community established its hope and its life. Once again, therefore, we shall be discussing Jesus' presence; but, this time, we shall also have to discuss his absence. For the early Christians were deeply conscious of the fact that he had "left" or, if you will, "returned" to the Father. This "departure," moreover, took on a very positive meaning, which concerned not only the person of Jesus but even the day-by-day life of the Christian community. What was this meaning? And how was it incorporated, more especially, into the central act of the assemblies: the celebration of the "Lord's Supper"?

Still, their acceptance of an absence of Jesus was counterbalanced by their certitude of a presence of the Spirit. How was this presence of the Spirit envisaged in relation to the life of the total Christian community? What was the global meaning of the principal images commonly used in speaking of it?

Lastly, as soon as we treat of Jesus' presence in the Christian community, we become particularly interested in the nature and extent of that same community's initial self-awareness. How did the early Church define herself, firstly and fundamentally, in order to recognize in herself an authentic presence of Jesus, beyond the Eucharist itself? This question will bring up the subject of Christian brotherhood. Indeed, Jesus' Eucharistic presence makes sense only if it rests on what we shall call his baptismal presence. Here, Christian brotherhood is the basic value which governs all the rest; and whenever it is overshadowed, the whole complexus of Christian values is in danger of disintegrating.

Toward the First Christian Assemblies

The first model of Jesus' activity was the
prophet, Yahweh's herald. In Israel, this model
was represented chiefly by the great names of Isaiah
and Jeremiah. From the social viewpoint, it immediately defined a certain type of presence and
suggested certain ways of thinking and doing which
were distinctive enough to guarantee that the general orientation of an activity, at the very least,
would become instantly perceptible around the
person who adopted them.

Above all, of course, the ancient and prestigious
model of Yahweh's herald suggested a special style
of utterance. From the lips of a herald, one expected a "message."

Jesus' Initial Message; Chance Listeners

Thus it is that Jesus wanted to go "all through
Galilee" first (Mk. 1, 39). By means of an image
which was very significant in those days—that of
the "kingdom of God"—he spread the "Good News"
that all the best and keenest and most desirable in
the hope of the past would soon be accomplished
(Mk. 1, 14-15). For the moment, then, he had to
work fast in order to cover *all of Galilee.*

Throughout this opening phase, which very
likely lasted several months, we must not visualize
Jesus as surrounded by regular gatherings or stable
audiences, to whom he could devote all his attention
for hours on end. By its nature, on the contrary,
the herald's message could reach only *chance lis-*

teners. If to that message we add the "signs"—cures
of all sorts—which underscored its global purport
with regard to hope; if, besides, we note his statements that he had a "mission"—and the synagogue services on the Sabbath could give him an
opportunity to say so (Lk. 4, 15-30)—then we can
fairly easily discern the broad outline of Jesus'
early activity.

The Message Planted a Seed

The message planted a seed but could not be
expected to make the harvest ripen immediately.
That Jesus knew. He does not seem to have worried
about it, either. What extraordinary assurance!
This trait of Jesus' early activity deserves to be
brought out for several reasons.

First, it reestablishes the truth of history. At
the same time, it corrects the conventional notion
that Jesus preached without letup from the beginning to the end of the Gospel event. The reality
was *different,* and it was also far less monolithic.
What is perhaps still richer in suggestion for our
pastoral and Christian programs is the happy dis-
covery that Jesus, in this first period, straightaway
accepted the delays of our individual and collective
conscience and even adjusted his whole enterprise
to something which he knew could mature only
with time.

So many of those who happened to hear the
initial message *would never again see* the herald
who, almost without their realizing it, had brought
them the "Good News" that all their hope be deci-
sively regenerated. And yet Jesus kept traveling like
this "all through Galilee." Apparently, he was less

worried than we—and less systematic, too. The profound and mirific slowness of germination did not frighten him (Mk. 4, 26-29). By this style, Jesus' evangelical activity paralleled, from the beginning, the long amplitudes of God's plan as it already shows through in the movement of creation itself.

Instruction: The First Stable Audiences

To all intents and purposes, Jesus did not have *stable audiences* until his utterance underwent a change of form from "message" to "instruction." After being a herald, Jesus became a "teacher" and surrounded himself with "disciples." This created a new situation, which, however, was not fixed once and for all. As a matter of fact, Jesus returned to the message later, when circumstances seemed to require it, and also when the progress of his instruction gave him relative freedom regarding his closest disciples (thus, among other texts, Mt. 9, 35; 11, 1 and Lk. 8, 1). In all this again, we must take notice of many nuances which are fairly often obscured in the picture we paint of Jesus' activity.

The Twelve

And, first, we should remember that the Twelve themselves did not become "apostles" from the moment they were counted in the forefront of Jesus' "disciples." These two titles referred, concretely, to statuses which differed greatly from one another (Mt. 10, 1-16 and par.). In their capacity as "disciples," the Twelve were Jesus' most constant listeners and, for that reason, the principal beneficiaries of his "instruction." They "followed" him wherever he went. Only after having acquired a certain familiarity with the thinking of their "teacher," therefore, could they normally receive a "mission" similar to his. This first "mission," moreover, seems to have been brief enough. At a certain stage, according to Luke, the Twelve *were not the only ones* to share this responsibility (Lk. 10, 1-20). At any rate, in their new capacity as *envoys,* or "apostles," they in turn adopted the herald's type of activity and mode of living. Then, they left their "teacher" and brought into new locales, not his "instruction," but his initial "message."

Beyond the Circle of the Twelve

On the other hand, we should not restrict all of Jesus' attention to the Twelve. Reaching beyond that more intimate circle, he spoke to a whole world of less assiduous "disciples," who, at the lowest level, were what our accounts simply call "crowds." This wider circle is where the women seem most naturally to have found their place (see, in particular, Lk. 8, 1-3). All in all, then, here was a pretty varied world of listeners, a world with ill-defined frontiers. On its outer rim, Jesus doubtlessly found a goodly number of secret sympathizers. But, since the boundaries of such groups always remained open, we must not be surprised, on the other hand, that his more resolute adversaries had little trouble working their way in.

The Twelve and the Subsequent Organization of the Church

Lastly, it is preferable not to be too hasty about

projecting onto the Twelve, right from the start, an image which, in reality, derives from a much later organization of the Church. It is certain, we believe, that when contemplating the more distant future of the Gospel event, Jesus gave a special place to the activity of the Twelve. It seems equally certain to us that, among them, Jesus entrusted a distinctive share of evangelical responsibility to the apostle Peter (Mt. 16, 18-19; Lk. 22, 31-32; Jn. 21, 15-17). But we would be stretching the point if, starting from these facts, we immediately viewed the Twelve as an "apostolic college," structured then and there like a "hierarchy" in action and armed with a clear distribution of powers. The real situation was considerably more fluid and, let us admit, closer to life. There is no evidence, particularly, that Jesus considered Peter a sort of prototype, henceforth thought of, among the Twelve, as chiefly responsible for the further spreading of evangelical hope. Only slowly and, to tell the truth, fairly late did these things become more definite under this form. Otherwise, there would be quite a problem accounting for the concrete modalities of the apostles' activity as the early Christian community actually experienced it.

Church and Assembly

All things considered, then, there never were regular "assemblies" around Jesus. There were "disciples," of varying status, around a "teacher" —which is something else. In reality, it was only after Jesus' departure that real "assemblies" could take shape in the first Christian communities.

The First Christian Assemblies

To be more precise, it seems that the "breaking of the bread" and the celebrating of the major "Eucharist," on set days, combined with an "instruction" which recalled that of Jesus, played a decisive role in the appearance of the first Christian assemblies (Acts 2, 42; *Didache* 9-10; 14, 1-3). In any case, I think there can be little doubt that it was assemblies of this sort which originally gave the Christian community its name of "church" *(ekklesia)*. It was also in these assemblies that Jesus' disciples, old and new, could from the first generation, be most intensely conscious of forming an original "brotherhood" whose most distinguishing characteristic flowed from a hope of "life" received in faith and shared in reciprocal love.

From then on, mutual aid in all its forms, and —at least in Jerusalem—a certain degree of common ownership made possible by pushing the old practice of almsgiving to the limit, became like so many fruits and concrete signs of their much more fundamental, interior sharing of *evangelical hope* (Acts 2, 44-45; 4, 32-35). Finally, it was by seeking to satisfy the many needs of its members, and especially of the assemblies themselves, that the Christian community gradually developed what we now call the "pastoral service" of the Church.

Jesus' Absence and Presence

My title—without its being too obvious, I admit

—was meant to pose a question concerning Jesus' *presence* in this Christian community whose early development we have just described. Yet, is "presence" really the right word to use here in preference to all others? Assuredly, it is the one which springs to mind first. Basing ourselves on our own vision of things, we readily imagine that the first Christian generation lived in profound awareness of a permanent presence of Jesus among his own.

Jesus' Absence

From a certain standpoint, that is undoubtedly true. We shall come back to it in a few moments. Still, there is reason to wonder whether this is the fact which should be given first place. Indeed, if we think of Jesus' *person,* it is clear that the early Christian community very strongly felt his *absence* rather than his presence. Perhaps we of today deceive ourselves a trifle on this subject.

More sensitive than we to Jesus' *humanity,* the first Christian generation was also, for this very reason, more attentive than we to the reality of his *departure* and, therefore, to the immediate implications of what has to be called his *absence.* Moreover, there is no need of scholarly reading between the lines to detect this feeling of absence in the apostolic writings we possess. No one even attempted to conceal it; quite the contrary, it was expressed as overtly as possible and in a hundred different ways.

We shall find the fourth Gospel an excellent witness here. *Departure* is one of the most insistent themes in Jesus' last conversations with his disciples. Now, there is no doubt that, at least in part, it is the Christian community itself which expressed its sentiments through these conversations. "Before the feast of the Passover, when Jesus"—notice the *name*—"when Jesus knew that his hour had come to *depart* out of this world to the Father, having loved his own who were *in the world,* he loved them *to the end*" (Jn. 13, 1—RSV). More explicitly still:

> My little children,
> I shall not be *with you* much longer.
> You will look for me,
> and, as I told the Jews,
> *where I am going,*
> *you cannot come* (13, 33).

"Simon Peter said, 'Lord where are you going?' Jesus replied, *'Where I am going* you cannot follow me *now;* you will follow me later'" (13, 36). Or this:

> I *am going* now to prepare a place for you,
> and after I *have gone* and prepared you a
> place,
> I *shall return* to take you with me;
> so that *where I am*
> you may be too.
> You know the way to the place where I *am*
> *going* (14, 2-4).

And lastly:

> If you loved me, you would have been glad
> to know
> that I *am going* to the Father (14, 28).

The Hope That Jesus Would Return

As we could conclude along the way, the hope that Jesus would *return*—a hope deeply anchored

in the consciousness of the early Christian community—presupposed the corresponding perception
of the fact that he was really *absent.*

> I will *come back* to you.
> In a short time the world will no longer see
> me;
> but *you will see me,*
> because I *live* and you *will live.*
> On that day
> you will understand that I *am in my Father*
> and you in me and I in you (Jn. 14, 18-20).

The "ascension" presented things in a more pal-
pable form, but its global significance was obviously
the same. It, too, united departure and return, in-
tervening absence and new presence: "Why are you
men from Galilee standing here looking into the
sky? Jesus"—notice the *name* again—"Jesus who has
been *taken up* from you into heaven, this same
Jesus *will come back* in the same way as you have
seen him *go there*" (Acts 1, 11).

The Eucharist: Jesus' Absence and Presence

A third witness to this sense of Jesus' absence
comes to us from a quarter where, admittedly, we
have more or less lost the habit of expecting it. It
is capital, however. I am all the more obliged to
call attention to it here as it touches upon the
innermost life of the first Christian *assemblies.*

This testimony is that of the *Eucharist.* We view
the Eucharist as the special locus of a permanent
presence of *Jesus* in the Christian community. And
once again, in a sense, we are right. However, I
do not believe that the early Christians would have
been as ready as we are to simply link such a pres-

ence with the very *person* of *Jesus*. When discussing the Eucharist, they originally spoke of the
"body" and the "blood" of Jesus: of his "body"
delivered up to death for us, and of his "blood"
shed as the sign of a new "covenant," or, if you
prefer, as the sign of a *new order of hope*. In both,
moreover, they saw precisely the supereminent sign
of this *hope of "life"* which, in the long run, was
identical with the essential significance of the
Gospel event. Besides, this was the very way Jesus
had expressed himself on the subject (1 Cor. 11,
23-27; Mk. 14, 22-25 and par.; compare Jn. 6, 34-58).

There is here, it seems to me, a distinction
which we cannot overlook without damaging the
profound equilibrium of our Christian consciousness. In any case, one thing is sure: what the assemblies of the apostolic generation felt most keenly,
in connection with the Eucharist itself, was an
absence rather than a presence. Understand me
correctly: it is *Jesus' person* which was then thought
of as absent.

Such, indeed, was the basic fact: Jesus was
really *gone*. His departure had a *meaning;* it represented a positive *value*. Far from denying this
value and diluting this meaning, the author of the
fourth Gospel, especially, took great care that they
should be grasped and accepted, as is clear from the
general orientation which he imprinted on Jesus'
last conversations with his disciples (Jn. 13-17).
The Eucharist, then, could take on its true meaning and assume its true value only in the *prolonga-
tion* of that basic fact: the *departure* of Jesus,
which, in the last analysis, was identified with his
entry into the glory of the resurrection.

The Eucharist Celebrated as an Expectation

For this reason, the Eucharist was first celebrated as an *expectation*. Its most direct meaning and value consisted in presenting to the assembly, in the bread and wine, the recognized signs of Jesus' "body" and "blood." These signs, in turn, guaranteed the assembly that its expectation was not in vain; they reminded it that the firmness of its hope would lead it, too, to "resurrection" and "life." Enveloped in "benediction" *(eukkaristia— eulogesis)*, they "proclaimed," in their own way, what was the very substance of the Gospel event (1 Cor. 11, 26).

Absent, Jesus had, indeed, been the *first* to map out, in his death and resurrection, *the most advanced road* of Christian hope. He *was* the "resurrection" and the "life" (Jn. 11, 25-26). The Eucharist *mapped out this same road* for the assembly once again. Thus, Jesus was there, absent and present at the same time: absent, because he had *returned* to the Father in order to prepare a place for us; and present, because his "body" and "blood," under the species of bread and wine, *truly mapped out anew* for the assembly the road which leads to the Father. So was it to be "until the Lord [came]" (1 Cor. 11, 26).

In a word, the Eucharist was celebrated, as people loved to say then, in "memory" of the Lord Jesus (1 Cor. 11, 24-25 and par.). But it could not have been a "memorial" unless the assembly had first attributed some meaning and value to Jesus' absence. This meaning and value was that Jesus was henceforth "glorified" with the Father. But, again, the Eucharist would not have been a "memorial" unless, correlatively, they had attributed equal truth to a certain presence of him who, under the signs of his "body" and "blood," retraced, for hope, the one road of "resurrection" and "life," "until his coming."

A Presence of Retracement

Jesus' Eucharistic presence among those who assembled for the "Lord's Supper" (1 Cor. 11, 20) could, then, be defined, from the viewpoint of the first Christian assemblies, as a *presence of retracement.* The Eucharist, in the assembly, actually retraced the road of evangelical hope. Moreover, such a presence resulted from the *whole* of the "Lord's Supper": first, from the brotherly assembly itself; and also, needless to say, from the "benediction," which accompanied the acts with the bread and the wine, and which proclaimed the meaning of these acts in words of praise addressed to God for the "wonders" he had wrought *principally* in Jesus, Christ and Lord, with a view to grounding the ultimate hope of "resurrection" and "life." Rather than a passive presence, this was plainly an *active* presence, by the very fact that the "Lord's Supper" once again traced out the road of the Gospel's decisive hope. Finally, as we have said, a presence of this sort rested on the very lofty meaning which was attached to Jesus' *departure,* and, thus, to his *absence,* "until he should return." All things considered, therefore, Jesus' Eucharistic presence was a *presence of the intermediate stage of hope,* just as the brotherly assembly itself, *at the same time,* served to signify and prepare the gathering of mankind into the great family of the "children of God, where Jesus had gone."

The Presence and Activity of the Spirit

I have stressed this early Eucharistic testimony because it underlines, with particular force, what was unquestionably one of the major elements in the consciousness of the first Christian communities. But, in compensation, there was "Another"—one who had *come* "to be with [us] forever" (Jn. 14, 16). This "Other" was the Spirit.

Jesus' Eucharistic Presence in the Concrete Dynamism of Christian Hope

In the West, especially since the Middle Ages, our pastoral endeavor, following in the wake of theology, strongly emphasized a Eucharistic *presence* of Jesus whose proper locus tended to be restricted to the sacramental signs of the "consecrated" bread and wine. According to this view, "consecration" created the presence. As we realize more and more today, it was too narrow a view of the much more complex reality of the "Lord's Supper." It was also a very static concept of our Eucharist.

From the standpoint which we are taking at this moment, we may ask whether such a concept of Jesus' *presence* among us did not finally introduce a serious disequilibrium in our entire Christian heritage. For there is certainly a connection—going back much further even than the Middle Ages—between the growth of this particular perception of Jesus' Eucharistic presence, on the one hand, and, on the other, the progressive obscurement, through the centuries, of the meaning and value of another perception: that of an *absence* of Jesus consequent upon his return to the Father.

What was most immediately affected, in this sort of reversal of perspectives, was the *concrete dynamism of Christian hope,* whose bases had, so to speak, changed poles. These matters are difficult to analyze, and it would be historically dangerous for us here to indulge in unnuanced affirmations. But the global fact seems to admit of no doubt.

Jesus' Eucharistic Presence and the Presence of the Spirit

I would add, furthermore, that there is probably a close—though obscure—correlation between the development of Jesus' Eucharistic presence as we generally conceive of it, and what must be termed a certain retrogression in our perception of the *presence of the Spirit* in the Christian community. This illustrates the difficulty of maintaining the proper balance between the principal constituents of our Christian hope. Still, that balance is what truly matters, above and beyond all the more or less divergent thrusts of which any value can be the object, at some time or other, independently of its authentic position in our total heritage.

A Certain Image of the Spirit

However that may be, it is quite certain that we are presently fostering a singularly impoverished and weak image of the Spirit's presence in the Christian community. Our very terminology, too, has worked against us here. When we say "Spirit" in the appropriate context, we almost immediately think of "Holy"; and this is far and away our most common formula: "Holy Spirit." Let us immediately note, however, that the early Christian community's vocabulary in this area was notably less uniform, and more flexible, more diversified and more suggestive. Besides "Holy Spirit," they also said "Spirit of God," "Spirit of Jesus" or simply "Spirit"—not to mention a goodly number of more ample formulas which did not primarily evoke the idea of "holiness."

When speaking of the Spirit, then, we almost invariably add "Holy." This is what seems significant to me. For, in our thinking, the "holy" here seems to mean principally the *morally holy,* the upright, the pure. And the "dove" appears reassuringly in the firmament of our minds! Thus more or less profoundly "moralized" (in keeping with a certain commandment morality), the image which spontaneously haunts our consciousness all too often makes us look upon the Spirit of God as a sort of interior mentor of our obedience and discipline as well as the supreme guarantor of the order established in us by the law. For the institution, the Spirit becomes the inviolable foundation stone of permanence and stability. A precious assurance, he is also something like the last invisible rampart against anarchy—or what we deem to be anarchy. In the same order of preoccupations, he offers us his assistance against error. This is the Spirit seen as the providential parapet of sound doctrine.

Our Authentic Heritage

These are caricatures? Exaggerations? I wish they were. But I am not so sure—at least in relation to a whole world of vague images which very efficaciously govern the concrete life of the Christian community. What freshness, at any rate, and what a change when we turn to our authentic heritage!

The Symbolism of the Dove

To be sure, the first generation of Christians was familiar with the dove used as a symbol to suggest participation by the Spirit of God in the Gospel event. Jesus' baptism (Mt. 3, 16 and par.) is such a familiar episode that I need not describe it in detail. However, we should not be too hasty about slanting this symbolism toward innocence, purification or even fecundity.[1] In point of fact,

---

[1] For this last suggestion, some capitalize on a comparison with Gen. 1, 2: "Now the earth was a formless void, there was darkness over the deep, and God's spirit [breath] hovered over the water" [less literally, the great and majestic sea breeze]. Those who propose this parallel are thinking of Jesus' baptism as the entrance into a "new creation." Needless to say, they are also thinking of a sort of prefigurative "sanctification" of the waters of Christian baptism. In itself, and with a few modifications, this could be a defensible view of the *ultimate* meaning of the Gospel event. But, at the time of this episode, Jesus' activity was just about to begin, and, therefore, we should be concerned with the *initial* meaning of the Gospel event. For that reason, the parallel with Gen. 1, 2 seems strained to me: it conflicts with the immediate context. We would be on a better path if we turned to the account of the flood (Gen. 8, 8-12). When the waters receded, the dove came back with nothing at first, but later returned with "a new olive-branch in its beak" and finally "returned . . . no more"—a testimony to the return of *God's favor*. The earth was inhabitable once again: this signified

it is far more concerned with reconciliation, peace and, in short, *God's favor* (Mt. 3, 17 and par.). The symbolism of the dove is, therefore, perfectly appropriate. As for its meaning, it is related to that which the ancient account of the flood had already utilized (Gen. 8, 8-12). Thanks to Jesus' activity, the forthcoming inauguration of the Gospel event would present itself, in effect, as an ever more decisive renewal of man's age-old *hope*.

The Wind and the Fire

It is also important to note that, in talking about the Spirit, the first generation of Christians did not confine themselves to the symbolism of the dove. In fact, when the Gospel event began to reveal its ultimate meaning, the image of the Spirit assumed another form—clearly situated (despite appearances) in the same area of significance as the first, and no less suggestive. This new image was that of wind and fire (Acts 2, 2; comp. 4, 31).

Here again, we should wisely distrust our desire for order and security. The wind of Pentecost was not an imperceptible breeze which would not have disturbed a straw; it was a "violent gust" which filled the entire house where the Twelve were gathered (Acts 2, 2). In an analogous situation, the disciples felt everything around them "rocking" (Acts 4, 31).

Neither was the fire those paradoxical large, motionless "drops" to which a certain brand of iconography has long since accustomed us, for the

the recommencement of *blessing* after the curse, of *hope* after ruin.

greater satisfaction of our taste for beautiful arrangements indefatigably stylized by the administration and the law. In the familiar imagery of Jewish antiquity, fire conjures up, not so much the slippers of security, as that active element which hungrily devours established situations and so marks the ruptures which announce fresh beginnings.

Power, Renewal, Creation and Life

I cannot devote more space to this analysis of images of the Spirit among the early Christians. What stands out, essentially, is that the Spirit, even when described as "holy," regularly and primarily suggests *power, renewal, creation* and *life*.[2] For this very reason, the Spirit is perceived as the unforeseeable power which presides over "new births" (Jn. 3, 4-8). Once we have become "sons of God," the Spirit dwells in each of us as the first witness to our adoption (Gal. 4, 6). The experience of his multiple gifts makes his testimony manifest. And in addition, throughout the period of our hope, the Spirit is like a first remittance on our heritage of "life" (Eph. 1, 14).

After that, it is hardly necessary to add that the Spirit is not reserved to those entrusted with serving the Christian community. He cannot be

[2] The Spirit is "holy" first of all because he comes *from God*. He is the *"imperishable* spirit [breath] of the living God" (Wis. 12, 1) —whence his direct connection with the *resurrection* of Jesus first, and, consequently, with the hope of a *resurrection similar to his* (Rom. 1, 4; 8, 11). In every order of things and values, we might say, the Spirit of God moves in the *same direction as life*, in order to lead it to its true goal, even beyond its most evident and immediate goal.

enclosed within the framework of any mode of government. Particularly significant in this regard is the narrative of the Acts of the Apostles. What a surge of creation and renewal! Everywhere, we see the Spirit of God—who is at the same time the Spirit of his Son—ensuring the *spread of evangelical hope* by the most diverse means, according to circumstances. At bottom, this is obviously what matters, rather than abstractly preserving more or less clearly defined jurisdictions (see, among other passages, the case of the Seven: Acts 6, 1-6; compare 6, 8-7, 53 and 8, 26-40). Furthermore, in the matter of "truth," the Spirit should not be thought of as a mere safeguard against error. More positively and more creatively, he is first and foremost that power which forges ahead in countless ways and leads the Christian community, step by step, to the full *significance* of the Gospel event (Jn. 14, 16; 16, 13). We must even admit that the Spirit freely crosses all the frontiers within which certain narrower views would like to hold him. No one is excluded. More astonishing still, a hope related to that of the Gospel seeks its way through the prodigious development of this human dwelling (Rom. 8, 18-25).

The Place of Christian Brotherhood in the Equilibrium of Our Gospel Heritage

We have stressed the fact that the first generation of Christians were deeply conscious of Jesus' departure and, therefore, of his absence, "until he should come." But we have also shown that they gave that absence an extremely positive value with regard both to Jesus himself and to the Christian community. We have likewise demonstrated that, from the viewpoint of the concrete equilibrium and dynamism of Christian hope, Jesus' absence was compensated by the experiential knowledge, so to speak, that the Spirit was permanently present. This Spirit was the Spirit both of the Father and of Jesus, Christ and Lord. To this Spirit belonged— first and foremost—power, renewal, creation and life. Therefore, the galvanic and multiform fostering of evangelical hope was directed, above all, to the free exercise of his activity.

A Presence of Jesus in Christian Brotherhood

It now remains for me to say a few words about a certain presence of Jesus in the Christian community insofar as this community originally saw itself as a *brotherhood*. But just what does brotherhood mean? Let me preface my answer with a remark which will surely seem quite negative at first. I do so only because, here again, I see the need of reopening the road to the recovery of certain values whose prolonged eclipse could throw our Christian heritage into a perilous disequilibrium.

Should We Consecrate the Expression: "The Church, the New People of God"?

Much has been said lately about the "people of God." This is incontestably a useful image if we are trying mainly to get a bird's-eye view of the Christian community as a whole. Up to a certain point, the image can be justified in itself; and, to a certain point also, it is authorized by very ancient use, going back even to the first generation of Christians.

Needless to say, moreover, it can fit in beautifully with hierarchical considerations. In today's parlance, "people" implies "nation," "nation" implies "government," and "government" implies "constitution" and the "sharing of powers." In the Church, "people of God" means "people" first, no doubt; but then it immediately implies "constitution" and "government" and, more specifically, "universal government" of the entire Christian community. All things considered, therefore, the notion of the Church as the "people of God" seems to put all its weight on the side of a *privileged* image of the universal Church and, thereby, on the side of the structures peculiar to her government.

Let us say straight out that we have nothing against this in principle. The universal Church is a very great reality; her government, at all levels, is also a reality—necessary, beneficial, and perfectly legitimate besides, under the proper conditions, from the viewpoint of what to us seems the best Christian tradition. That is not the question. Rather, what I would want to say here, in passing, is that I experience some difficulty in sharing the hope of those who hail the idea of the "people of God" as a radical remedy for the danger of clericalization in the Church. Under the present circumstances, words of this kind seem to possess a massive force before which all explanations could very well disintegrate in the long run, precisely because of their inevitable subtlety.

The Meaning and Limits of This Expression in the Early Christian Community

In any case, it would be impossible for me to admit, without nuances, that the early Christian community viewed itself, *first* and *fundamentally,* as the "people of God." Those who favor this opinion—and they are numerous at the present time—have not yet succeeded, to my mind, in giving it a solid exegetical basis. The paucity of apostolic texts which they are forced to fall back on does not seem to trouble them unduly—an indication whose warning we should not neglect.

Nevertheless, it is true that the early Christian community sometimes "defined" itself as the "people of God," though the "definition" was not always very explicit. But the whole point is that such a definition appears only in those fairly *exceptional* moments when the early Christian community was trying to situate itself *in regard to Israel* viewed as the "people of God." In this line of thinking, it was not at all inconceivable that, after some development at least, the young Church should come to see herself as the *true* "Israel" and the *true* "people of God."[3] For the early Christians, this was a way of marking both continuity and discontinuity in regard to Israel, from which they knew they had sprung. In this relation of continuity and discontinuity, there was a genuine problem

[3] See especially Gal. 6, 16: "the Israel of God"; Rom. 9, 14-33; 2 Cor. 6, 16; Tit. 2, 14; Heb. 8, 6-13; 1 Pet. 2, 9-10; Rev. 21, 3. It will be noted that all these passages, except the first, are based on quotations from the "scriptures" (for us, the Old Testament!).

of internal identity and of relationship to "the other," as the end of the story shows much more clearly yet.

How It Was First Used

At times, there was simply no way to evade this problem. After all, in the eyes of the apostolic generation, whether of pagan or Jewish origin, the "Old Testament" was still simply "the scriptures." These "scriptures" were read regularly at the assemblies of the Christian community and were constantly utilized in every form of service of the word. What is really significant, under these circumstances, is not that the early Christian community more or less clearly perceived itself, and more or less expressly defined itself several times, as the new "people of God," in whom the promises made to the old were being fulfilled; but rather that, in the final analysis, this perception and definition do not seem to have occupied *a greater place* in the global consciousness which the early Church could have of herself at that time. Thus we reach a conclusion which is almost contrary to what the current opinion presupposes.

To Define Itself, the Early Christian Community Turned, Fundamentally, in Another Direction

Furthermore, it is hard to believe *a priori* that the early Christians, individuals as well as assemblies, devoted most of their thinking to themselves so as to resolve the problem of their inner identity *in terms of their relationship to an "Israel" seen as the "people of God."* Concretely, "the Jews" gave the apostolic generation far more persistent and pressing matters to consider. Still and all, such a preoccupation could arise naturally enough among Christians of Jewish descent. Consider the case of Paul himself (especially Rom. 9-11). But the question must have seemed much less urgent to Christians come over from paganism. In this connection, we must not forget that the entire collection of apostolic writings, unless I am mistaken, is of Jewish origin. Quite normally, then, their testimony on this precise subject bears the mark of their origin. In actual fact, however, everything indicates that the consciousness of the early Christian community was, from the start, oriented mainly in another direction, largely independent of a massive identification with what woud have presented itself as a new "people of God."

The Testimony of the Vocabulary of Christian Brotherhood

On this point, according to sound methodology, I believe that we are obliged to rely chiefly on the testimony of the vocabulary which was *most commonly used*. Now, for anyone who reads the apostolic writings attentively, one fact soon stands out with particular clarity. It is the extraordinary abundance of the vocabulary of Christian *brotherhood*. So cogent is the evidence in this regard that we need not pause for a long demonstration.

"Brother" and "Sister": Two Common Titles among the Early Christians

The first Christians regularly called one another "brother" and "sister." "Greetings to Asyncritus ... Hermas, and all the *brothers* who are with them" (Rom. 16, 14). "Erastus, the city treasurer, sends his greetings; so does our *brother* Quartus" (Rom. 16, 23). "I commend to you our *sister* Phoebe" (Rom. 16, 1). "From Paul . . . and from our *brother* Timothy; to our dear fellow worker Philemon, our *sister* Apphia . . ." (Phm. 2). "One day Peter stood up to speak to the *brothers* . . ." (Acts 1, 15). "Think of God's mercy, my *brothers* . . . I beg you" (Rom. 12, 1).

A Custom Which Must Have Gone Back to Jesus Himself

It is extremely probable that this custom went back to Jesus himself. "Simon . . . once you have recovered, you in turn must strengthen your *brothers*" (Lk. 22, 32). "[Mary,] go and find the *brothers* [or "my *brothers*"]" (Jn. 20,17). "Anyone who is angry with his *brother* . . ." (Mt. 5, 22). "You, however, must not allow yourselves to be called Rabbi, since you have only one master, and you are all *brothers*" (Mt. 23, 8). Moreover, this manner of viewing and expressing the *fundamental* bond of the community subsisted fairly long in the early Church. Toward the middle of the second century, Justin mentions the baptismal rite and expressly states, "Then we lead [the newly baptized] into the assembly of those whom we call *brothers*" (1 *Apology*, 65). Indeed, only with the birth and flowering of monasticism—that is, in the third and fourth centuries—did this venerable custom, already weakened, begin to be restricted to particular "communities," distinct and more or less separated from the basic community. This trend toward a particularizing of Christian brotherhood even today finds its chief expression in the multitude of "religious communities."

Brotherhood: A Treasure of the Christian Community

It was not so in the beginning. On the contrary, brotherhood was at once considered *a treasure of the Christian community as such,* a treasure shared equally by each and every member. It embodied the first claim to the entire baptismal heritage. Thus, where this heritage was concretely shared, *there was the "Church."* Therefore, it is in brotherhood so conceived, rather than in the more remote idea of a new "people of God," that we must *first* look for the image through which the early Christian community perceived and defined itself. As a matter of fact, the *multiple values* which constituted brotherhood made up the fabric of *everyday* Christian consciousness, for the "assemblies" *(ekklesiai)* as well as for the individuals who took part in them, according to the requirements of the moment. Furthermore, this same awareness of forming a "brotherhood" distinguished the Christian community from "outsiders," whoever they were (1 Thess. 4, 12; 1 Cor. 5, 12-13; Col. 4, 5).

The Title of "Brother" Was Not Reserved to Members of the Local Church

It is important to stress, in addition, that the title of "brother" was by no means reserved to members of the local Church. Not the result of mere *sociological* elbow rubbing, it was a title *without boundaries* throughout the *whole* of the Christian community. It enjoyed the same universality, so to speak, as the welcome given to the hope which the Gospel held forth. "There is one Body, one *Spirit,* just as you were all called into one and the same *hope* when you were called. There is one *Lord,* one faith, one *baptism,* and one God who is *Father of all,* over all, through all and within all" (Eph. 4, 4-6). With an admirable wealth of suggestion, this text proclaims the fundamental values which composed Christian brotherhood. Essentially, then, they were what determined and shaped one's adherence. The text also indicates that, this being so, the only restrictions which could be placed on the title of "brother" depended, in the last analysis, on the welcome which the individual felt he could give to the hope found in the Gospel.

A Brotherhood Spread throughout the World

Disembarking one day at Puteoli, on the Gulf of Naples, Paul and his companions experienced the joy of finding some "brothers," who immediately offered them hospitality (Acts 28, 14). Now, at that time, Paul was making his first personal contacts with the Christian communities of Italy. Shortly after, the "brothers" of the Church at Rome surrounded him with the same attentions (Acts 28, 15-16). Christians, wherever they were and wherever they went, looked upon one another as members of one *same brotherhood,* spread to every corner where the Gospel message had been heard.

But it is still more curious to observe, in this connection, that the first epistle of Peter, in which some profess to find the most explicit testimony on the Church as the new "people of God" (2, 9-10), views the Christian community no less explicitly under the more familiar image of a "brotherhood." "Honor all men. Love the *brotherhood*.... [Remain] firm in your faith, knowing that the same experience of suffering is required of *your brotherhood* throughout the world" (2, 17; 5, 9—RSV; *adelphotes* in both cases).

The Church, the New People of God: A Secondary Image

Of these two images—the "people of God" and a local and universal "brotherhood"—which one was, at that time, truly primary and fundamental? Whatever may have been said on the subject, especially in the last few years, the answer to this question seems clear to me, provided we do not project more recent preoccupations on the early Christian community. That community, *in its most intimate everyday life,* looked upon itself first and foremost as a "brotherhood." And if, at times, it also looked upon itself as the new "people of God," that was at the much rarer moments when it was compelled to situate itself, in diverse ways, *with regard to the totality of values which the people of Israel in its capacity as a people had represented and still did represent.* Compared with the image of a "brotherhood," that of the new "people of God" is *secondary,* just as the occasional images of "temple of God" and "body" or "spouse" of Christ are also secondary.

The Church as a Brotherhood Refers to the Basic Community First

This conclusion, as can well be imagined, carries with it numerous and far-reaching consequences. It suggests a style of ecclesial life. It also suggests a definite orientation for pastoral activity and Christian living. Indeed, if "brotherhood" is the point at issue, the principal questions which will be asked about it more and more will concern the *basic community*. This community is the original and normal place where Christian brotherhood can be seen, developed, and lived to the full. It would be naive to think that we shall be able to dispense with its mediation. The key to an authentic renewal of the Church today is found in this basic community, which, by the nature of things, is the proper setting for the birth and growth of Christian brotherhood.

What should this basic community be? A place where our pastoral service will unwittingly and unwillingly continue to create Christian anonymity because of structures which, having abolished all genuine community, render words and sacraments anemic? Or, on the contrary, a place where our entire Christian heritage, with all its force of contestation and creation, will be efficaciously shared by men and women who, in the face of their brothers, can recognize the very face of Jesus, present in this way among them?[4] This is the great question, and it becomes more urgent every day as the old structures—parishes and dioceses—swell or crumble, under the combined pressure of demographic growth and the accelerated urbanization of our planet.

---

[4] It is hardly necessary to recall Jesus' well-known axiom here: "Insofar as you did this to one of the least of these *brothers of mine,* you did it to me" (Mt. 25, 40; see also, in a kindred sense, 1 Jn. 3, 16-18).

This is not the time to expatiate on the many questions which we have just raised. By way of conclusion, however, I think it useful to open up, here and now, several avenues of reflection. Circumstances are pushing us on extremely fast, so that we must immediately revive certain values of our Christian heritage which have long since fallen into a dangerous and frightening lethargy. These values concern, first of all, the *relationship of brotherhood* which each of us possesses in virtue of his baptism, and, at the same time, the fundamental perception that Jesus is *actively present* in the Christian community.

The Idea of a Basic Community

If we are truly "God's children" (1 Jn. 3, 1) and, consequently, can say that our God is the "Father *of all*" (Eph. 4, 6), with the result that we make "no more distinctions between Jew and Greek, slave and free, male and female" (Gal. 3, 28), it immediately follows that, assembled "into a house where God lives" (Eph. 2, 22), we must be brought—slowly but surely—to recognize the very face of Jesus, "the eldest of many brothers" (Rom. 8, 29), in the face of those few whom *we can know* by name. It becomes clear, then, that a basic experience is imperative here: that of *relationship* to "another" person, who, by the twofold title of creation and the Gospel, is recognized as a "brother." From this point of view, without a name there can be no brotherhood—not even human and, still less, Christian. Our love goes out *first* to the brother whom we can *see* (1 Jn. 4, 20). Accordingly, he is

the prime object of the evangelical "commandment" of brotherly love (Jn. 13, 34-35).

If, then, the basic structures of the Christian
community are set up in such a way that they most
often produce, not a "name," but anonymity—not
the "brother that [we] can see," but the "brother"
who is lost for us in the crowd, even though this
"crowd" has gathered for the Eucharistic celebration—then, *the indispensable and primary establishment of a relationship to the "other," recognized
as our "brother," will, by that very fact, be jeopard-
ized or perhaps made totally and forever impossible.*

Under such circumstances, how can we still
speak of a "Christian community" unless, like
ostriches, we bury our heads in illusion? At baptism, we all have a *name:* "Joseph—or Therese—
what do you seek in the Church of God?" But, with
few exceptions, we *no longer have a name* at the
"Lord's table," which, nevertheless, is both the sign
and the principal sustenance of our unity, *within
our brotherly relationship.* A strange situation, indeed, since it places us in complete institutional
contradiction at the very heart of our Christian
heritage! What has happened? The hope or, rather,
the *promise of brotherhood* included in our baptismal heritage has been lost along the way in the
sands of this anonymity which seems to have become the rule at most of our Eucharistic assemblies
throughout the world. What is to blame? Surely
not just the individual's poor understanding or ill
will. There is no use trying to explain all this by
sin; and, consequently, there is no use trying to
remedy the condition with glib exhortations to

virtue. When all the factors have been weighed, we are forced to ask some questions about the concrete setup of the fundamental structures of the Christian community.

This is what I meant a moment ago when I alluded to the problem presented by our basic community. *Reconstructing* this community in accordance with its specific needs and objectives is, I believe, one of the clearest and most urgent tasks facing the Church today. If our Christian and pastoral programs are to tie in once again—truly and vitally—with Jesus' evangelical program, we must start out from this reconstruction.

How shall we define the basic community in Christianity? Very briefly, I would say this: in the complex of structures within the Church, the basic community is *the necessary place for the primal and indispensable establishment of that brotherly relationship which unites all Christians among themselves.* It is likewise the proper place for *first transmitting and sharing* the substance of our Christian heritage. In its turn, our Christian heritage is defined, first and above all, by the hope of the Gospel. Now, since Jesus' resurrection, this hope has a name which we know: it is called "life," and, ultimately, "eternal life." From being the proper place for the initial forming of our brotherly relationship, therefore, the basic community becomes the spiritual scene of our *common* birth to this hope of "life" which is offered *to all* in the Gospel event. Its most distinctive acts, of course, are none other than baptism and the Lord's Supper: special—but by no means exclusive—signs of all the other *sharing* which form the dynamic framework of the Christian community itself.

The Frontiers of the Basic Community

On the other hand, the very term "basic community" shows quite clearly that this is not the only structure in the Church. How far does it extend, then? The basic community is the place where each Christian should normally have his initial opportunity to bear a "name," in the full sense of the word, within a relationship of brotherhood which itself is immediately consequent upon the common filiation of all "God's dispersed children" throughout the world. Thus, where the concrete possibility of *each individual's bearing a brotherly name* ends, there the basic community also ends. The boundaries of the basic community, therefore, are determined by the effective possibility for each of its members to acquire a "name" which is truly *a name of Christian brotherhood.*

Beyond this effective possibility, we proceed by degrees to vaster structures which, finally, envelop the universal brotherhood of all Christians. Clearly, then, there is a question of number here—but, just as clearly, not an abstract number. In actual practice, the number of Christians in the same basic community may vary. Still, the variation must not be left to chance. Here is the rule to apply: the size of the basic community should never be such that, to all intents and purposes, it destroys the concrete possibility for each member to have, in the eyes of his "brothers," an authentically brotherly "name," *continuous in some way with that of*

Jesus himself, who is thus present in the Christian community sprung from the Gospel.

Parish and Diocese

Now, among the present structures of the Church, neither the territorial parish nor especially the diocese can claim to fill the role of basic communities efficaciously. From the viewpoint of the integrity and fecundity of our Christian heritage as well as from the original viewpoint of Jesus' Gospel program—"gathering God's dispersed children into unity"—this powerlessness to create brotherhood undoubtedly constitutes, in the actual setup, the most radical defect of both institutions. At this point, each reader may analyze the situation for himself, according to what has just been said about the basic community. *Because of the inadequacy of structures which we have been content to receive passively from the past, the initial establishment of a brotherly relationship is, in general, no longer being assured in the Church.* Long since caught up in the anonymity of that phenomenon called the "crowd," at the very level of its most decisive attitudes and acts, the Christian community manages at best to perceive itself as a "people" (the Christian people, the people of God), with all the ambiguous consequences which such a perception can foster with regard to the *situating* of *services* and the *style of governing* in the general equilibrium of the values of our Christian heritage.

The only solution, it seems to me, is to re-create in the Church, at all costs and as soon as possible, a basic community capable of reestablishing genu-

ine Christian brotherhood among us—short of
which, discontent, sterility and dispersion will continue to gnaw at us, despite all attempts to reform
and all efforts to achieve closeness.

The Title of Brotherhood Enjoys Primacy over the Title of Service

The basic community which we are discussing
draws its inspiration from the most original and
solid creations of the early Christians. Needless to
say, much would remain to be done in order to
adapt the ancient idea to conditions in our era.
For instance, it would be necessary, from the start,
to provide the basic community with the organization and pastoral service best suited to its needs and
specific objectives.[5] It would also be necessary to
devise means of integrating the basic community
into the local community (village, city, area and
nation) and, through it, into the universal Christian community. In any case, at every level of this
manifold organization, the essential concern is that
the relationship of brotherhood acquired in the
basic community should not be lost as real contacts
become rarer and responsibility for services expands.

The first Christian communities seem to have
understood these matters fairly well. Thus, *in order
to safeguard brotherhood,* they spontaneously gave
the primacy *to their baptismal title,* which was common to all, *over the title of service,* which was special to a few. Even in the third century, for example,
Dionysius of Alexandria described the priest as

---

[5] On this last point, see *Structures of Christian Priesthood,*
pp. 93-105.

"a *brother* who [by his service] is counted in the ranks of the priests." This simple definition illustrates surpassingly well the original equilibrium between brotherhood and service. The title of "brother" comes first. In Christianity, there is none greater, since it derives immediately from our fundamental title of "God's children." Whatever more or less enduring prestige they may have acquired in the course of history, *all titles of service are secondary* to this initial title of brotherhood, which gathers us all into the "house of our God" and which alone opens the door to the hope offered us by the Gospel.

The Evangelical Values of Christian Brotherhood and Jesus' Presence in the Community

This Christian brotherhood should not be simplistically identified with a vague, romantic notion of togetherness or with some familial nostalgia, though perhaps, on the other hand, we should not be too quick to discredit these humble signs of our deepest spiritual needs. What we are talking about now is that brotherhood of which the early Christian community gave us an example, in the particular historical conditions in which it found itself.

In point of fact, we cannot renounce brotherhood any more than we can renounce the Gospel. For brotherhood flows from the substance of the Gospel. It flows from our God, whom we have been taught to call "Father." It flows from Jesus, who has shown us the way to him. It flows from the Spirit, who continues to ensure, throughout human history, the spread of the hope contained in the Gospel. It flows from our baptism, it flows from our common adoption, it flows from our conviction that we already share the hope of "resurrection" and "life" with all "God's dispersed children" in the world. Moreover, a certain concrete organization of the early Christians' brotherhood is what enabled them to understand that Jesus was somehow *present in their midst* as the "eldest of my brothers."

*

We are at a crossroads, the like of which we have probably never seen in our long past. The choices will be difficult and often painful. But they will not be less painful or less difficult if we turn our head so as not to face them. Today as well as yesterday, Jesus' presence in the Christian community does not result automatically from repeating the baptismal rite. And let us not be in too great a hurry to take refuge in the quietude of a certain Eucharistic presence of Jesus' in order to compensate for the void in our Christian brotherhood.

Jesus' Presence and the Implementation of Christian Brotherhood

For all these things go hand in hand. Jesus' *Eucharistic presence* presupposes his *baptismal presence,* and his baptismal presence, in turn, presupposes a *brotherhood* in which it takes shape. Christian brotherhood itself depends on conditions which are special to it. In order to be meaningful and effective, it requires *concrete modes of implementation;* but these are not, in themselves, given to us once and for all by unique and intangible models. Here is where we are being awaited: at the decisive point of truth and creation. The Spirit of the living God must, it seems, move in the direction of life.